Abortion

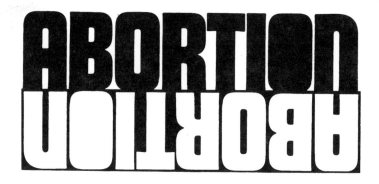

ABORTION

**Rights,
Options, and
Choices**

*Tricia
Andryszewski*

Issue and Debate

*The Millbrook Press, Inc.
Brookfield, Connecticut*

Photographs courtesy of Impact Visuals: pp. 10 (Tory Read), 40 (Greta Pratt), 46 (Marilyn Humphries), 55 (Tom McKitterick), 58 (Harvey Finkle), 66 (Jim Brozek), 75 (Harvey Finkle), 84 (Tory Read), 87 (Steve Wewerka), 95 (Jerome Friar), 101 (Marilyn Humphries); Wide World Photos: pp. 13, 29; Culver Pictures: p. 17; Bettmann: pp. 19, 22, 33, 61, 97; Louis DeLuca, JB Pictures: p. 83.

Library of Congress Cataloging-in-Publication Data
Andryszewski, Tricia, 1956–
Abortion : rights, options, and choices / Tricia Andryszewski.
p. cm. — (Issue and debate)
Includes bibliographical references and index.
Summary: Examines the changing legal, medical, and moral issues surrounding abortion before and since Roe v. Wade; considers both anti-abortion and pro-choice points of view.
ISBN 1-56294-573-4
1. Abortion—Law and legislation—United States—Juvenile literature. [1. Abortion.] I. Title. II. Series.
KF3771.Z9A53 1996
344.73'04192—dc20
[347.3044192] 95-42122 CIP AC

Published by The Millbrook Press, Inc.
2 Old New Milford Road, Brookfield, Connecticut 06804

Contents

Abortion

1

Violence and Controversy

"A man came in with a black duffel bag," an eyewitness later recalled. "He took out a rifle. He said, 'Is this Preterm?' The woman answering the phone said 'Yes,' and he dropped the bag and opened fire." [1]

The gunman, John C. Salvi III, shot and killed the receptionist, Leanne Nichols, at the Preterm Health Services Clinic in Brookline, Massachusetts. Minutes earlier, he had opened fire at a nearby Planned Parenthood facility, killing Shannon Elizabeth Lowney, a receptionist there. Five others were wounded in the two incidents. Salvi was arrested the next day, after he fired more than twenty rounds from his semiautomatic rifle at a clinic in Norfolk, Virginia, an incident in which fortunately no one was wounded.

The shootings in Massachusetts, on December 30, 1994, came on the heels of hundreds of violent incidents at places where abortions are performed. In recent years, abortion providers have been the targets of arson, bombing, stalking, assault, sabotage, burglary, and murder.

Since the 1970s, abortion has been a very
controversial issue throughout the United
States. Anti-abortion and pro-choice
organizations often express their differences
of opinion in lawful demonstrations. Some
individuals, however, express their views
through acts of violence.

A Long-Running Debate. For most of the twentieth century, most abortions were illegal in the United States. Hundreds of thousands of women had them nonetheless, and many died or were maimed by unlicensed abortionists operating under unsafe conditions. By the 1960s, many medical practitioners and women's advocates were speaking out in favor of making abortion legal.

In 1973 the U.S. Supreme Court, in *Roe* v. *Wade,* decreed that a constitutional "right to privacy" gives women the right to choose whether or not to bear children, and that this right includes a legal right to have an abortion. This decision has made it legal for women to seek abortions during the early part of pregnancy, before the fetus is capable of surviving on its own.

Many people have applauded *Roe* v. *Wade;* others have viewed it as a license to kill unborn children. In the 1970s, people who believed that abortion was murder began to form organizations opposing the practice. The anti-abortion movement grew in size and influence during the 1980s, as Presidents Ronald Reagan and George Bush and other prominent national leaders spoke out against abortion.

Some anti-abortion activists have staffed telephone hotlines intended to persuade pregnant women not to have abortions. Others have lobbied state legislatures to pass laws restricting abortion. Thousands have participated in actions at facilities where abortions are performed or at the homes of people who work at these facilities: picketing, talking with or shouting at women approaching the facility, handing out literature. Some have committed acts of civil disobedience to protest abortion and shut down abortion facilities, typically by illegally blocking access.

Anti-abortion protesters have also committed acts of violence. Vandalism, bomb threats, and death threats are commonplace at facilities across the country, and dozens of actual bombings have occurred. Arson and bombing attacks on abortion clinics began in the 1970s and increased in the 1980s. The personal threat to abortion providers has increased as well. In 1982, a Michigan doctor who performed abortions and his wife were kidnapped and held for a week before being released by several men who called themselves the Army of God. In the 1990s, the violence included the murders of personnel who provide abortions.

Judy Widdicombe, whose abortion clinic in St. Louis opened up soon after the *Roe* decision, describes how anti-abortion activism has escalated over the years:

> The day we opened Reproductive Health Services, we had pickets, but it was peaceful, sidewalk picketing. . . . For the first four or five years, we had pickets daily, but they stayed on the sidewalks and didn't do anything aggressive.
>
> It was in the late seventies that we began to see militant anti-choice activists like Joe Scheidler [founder of the Pro-Life Action League]. . . . By 1985, we were the site for an action by a militant anti-choice group; there were about three hundred people at the clinic from some fifteen states, and I remember sixty-one arrests.
>
> Bomb threats and death threats, which began in the early 1970s, got worse. I got death threats by mail. I got them in the middle of the night. People called on the phone and said, 'You dirty baby killer. You're going to die. I'd be careful getting in my car tomorrow morning if I were you.' . . .

*John C. Salvi III was accused of killing
two people in a Massachusetts
abortion clinic and shooting into
a clinic in Norfolk, Virginia.*

In June of 1986, after we had opened a second clinic site . . . we were firebombed.[2]

Spokesmen for anti-abortion organizations have insisted that the perpetrators of violence are individuals whose violent acts are not sanctioned by the anti-abortion movement. To the contrary, pro-choice activists (those who wish to preserve each woman's right to choose whether or not to have an abortion) insist that the anti-abortion movement has at the very least failed to condemn acts of violence *convincingly,* and has perhaps actively conspired to encourage them.

Two Years, Five Deaths. In March 1993, David Gunn, a physician who performed abortions at the Pensacola Women's Medical Services clinic in Florida, was shot to death by Michael F. Griffin, an anti-abortion activist. Griffin was convicted of first-degree murder and sentenced to life in prison.

In August of that year, George Tiller, a physician who performed abortions at a clinic in Wichita, Kansas, was shot and wounded as he left his clinic. The woman who fired the shots, anti-abortion activist Rachelle "Shelly" Shannon, was convicted of attempted murder.

In July 1994, John B. Britton, a physician who performed abortions, and James Barrett, his unarmed escort, were both shot to death outside the Ladies Center, in Pensacola, Florida. Barrett's wife, June, who was in a pickup truck with the two when they were shot, survived the shotgun barrage. Paul Hill, an anti-abortion activist, was convicted of both murders and sentenced to die in the electric chair.

In November 1994, Garson Romalis, a physician who performed abortions in Vancouver, British Columbia, just across the Canadian border from the state of Washington, was shot and wounded while eating breakfast at his home.

At the end of December 1994, John C. Salvi III opened fire in Massachusetts.

2

Before
Roe *v.* Wade

In the beginning, early abortion was legal in America. The earliest American law on abortion was based on British common law, which, until 1803, did not view abortion as a crime if it occurred before the fetus "quickened" (before the woman first felt the fetus move). Abortion after quickening was considered a serious offense, but not a capital crime like murder.

The first U.S. anti-abortion activists, in the 1800s, were physicians, formally trained members of medical associations dedicated to the practice of "scientific medicine." (Up until the 1800s, abortions had been performed primarily by midwives and practitioners of folk medicine.) These physicians, as part of their campaign to gain exclusive control of all U.S. medical care, declared that "quickening" was an ignorant superstition and that abortion at any stage of development was wrong. They lobbied for state laws against abortion and for state regulation of the practice of medicine in general.[1]

The physicians' campaign against abortion accelerated after the Civil War. By the late 1860s, many Prot-

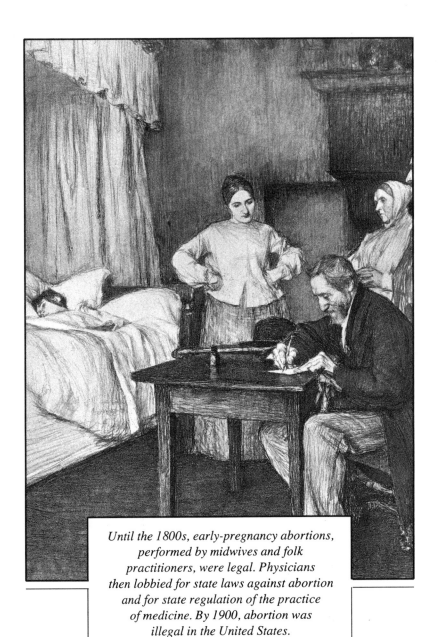

Until the 1800s, early-pregnancy abortions, performed by midwives and folk practitioners, were legal. Physicians then lobbied for state laws against abortion and for state regulation of the practice of medicine. By 1900, abortion was illegal in the United States.

estant churches as well as the Roman Catholic Church had joined in the anti-abortion movement. In 1873, Congress passed the Comstock Law (named after the young New York morality crusader Henry Comstock), which made it illegal to traffic in devices or medicines used for birth control or abortion. By 1900, abortion was illegal throughout the United States, except in cases where a physician deemed it necessary to save a mother's life.

Dangers and Difficulties. After birth control and abortion became illegal, there was an upsurge in deaths and injuries from clandestine abortions. Margaret Sanger, a passionate early advocate of making contraception freely available, describes the circumstances that drove her to defy the law and open the first U.S. birth-control clinic, in Brooklyn, New York, in 1916:

> On Saturday nights I have seen groups of fifty to one hundred women going into questionable offices well known in the community for cheap abortions. I asked several women what took place there, and they all gave the same reply: a quick examination, a probe inserted into the uterus and turned a few times to disturb the fertilized ovum, and then the woman was sent home. Usually the flow began the next day and often continued for four or five weeks. Sometimes an ambulance carried the victim to the hospital for a curettage, and if she returned home at all she was looked upon as a lucky woman.
> This state of things became a nightmare with me.[2]

Because of increasing health risks to women undergoing illegal abortions, Margaret Sanger (1883-1966) established the United States' first birth control clinic in New York City in 1916.

From the turn of the century through the 1960s, abortions were common in the United States, though most of them were illegal. Although the law was an ever-present and potent threat, it was relatively rare for a doctor to be prosecuted for abortion, and many doctors were quite lenient about agreeing to perform them. The decision was the doctor's, however—not the patient's—and most doctors did refuse. The conditions under which abortions were performed varied, from the safety and privacy of the office of a trusted family physician to the kitchen of an abortionist with no formal medical training. Poor women and rural women typically got the worst treatment.

Many years after the event, one woman—a self-supporting teacher whose husband had abandoned her—recalls her experience with abortion in the 1920s:

> We all knew where to go. There was quite an underground, if you can call it that, of women talking among themselves. If you were lucky, you found a real doctor, but it wasn't just the doctors who were doing abortions. The woman who performed mine was a nurse, I think. That was my hope at least. I wasn't allowed to ask for credentials, so I never knew. It was painful, I remember that, but reasonably safe, thank God.[3]

Medical care for Americans generally improved dramatically through the first half of the century, but medical conditions for the many women who sought abortions remained grim. Judy Widdicombe, who worked as a nurse in hospitals in the 1950s and 1960s, recalls:

> Abortion was not discussed then. I went through nursing school in the fifties, and it was

not discussed; neither was contraception. In the hospitals, they were doing abortions safely, but under the guise of something else. It was not uncommon to work in the operating room and have doctors doing 'D&Cs' [dilation of the cervix and curettage of the uterus], when you knew darn well they were doing early abortions.

I saw the privileged who could pay for it, who were educated and determined enough to make the system work for them, getting abortions. . . . [Other] women came in on GYN wards with all sorts of conditions and you suspected—even though they would maybe never admit it—that there had been an illegal abortion. There were a lot of kidney problems, bladder problems, and infections from incomplete abortions, where fragments of tissue were left inside. Many women died from peritonitis, an infection in the abdomen, and septicemia, an infection in the bloodstream.

Absolutely, all the time, women were pressured to give the names of the abortionists. . . . In those days, the authorities reported an abortion just like it was a major crime. . . . Usually, whoever was on duty in the emergency room—a nurse, a doctor, somebody, there was not much of a protocol—would call the police. Then, they would come and interrogate the woman.[4]

The case of Sherri Finkbine, mother of four children and host of *Romper Room*, a popular children's television program, attracted attention nationwide and highlighted what many Americans had come to see as shortcomings in U.S. laws on abortion. Sherri Finkbine

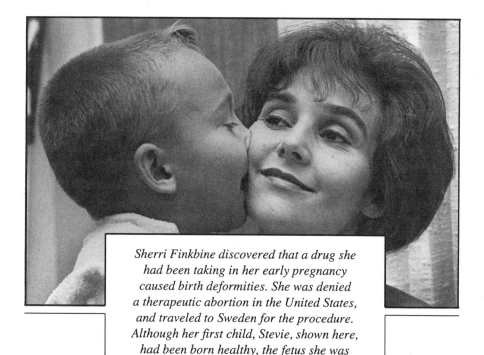

Sherri Finkbine discovered that a drug she had been taking in her early pregnancy caused birth deformities. She was denied a therapeutic abortion in the United States, and traveled to Sweden for the procedure. Although her first child, Stevie, shown here, had been born healthy, the fetus she was carrying was in fact seriously deformed.

occasionally used small doses of tranquilizers. In the early weeks of her fifth pregnancy, in 1962, she several times used a new tranquilizer that her husband had brought home from London the year before. Soon afterward, the Finkbines learned that the tranquilizer, thalidomide, had caused terrible deformities in the children of mothers who had taken it during pregnancy. Horrified, they sought a therapeutic abortion but were refused permission in state after state. Ultimately, Sherri Finkbine had to travel to Sweden for an abortion. After her abortion, she learned that the fetus had in fact been severely deformed.

Although it seems cruel that doctor after doctor refused the Finkbines an abortion in such difficult circumstances, the reality was that abortion was a serious crime that was dangerous for a doctor to commit. Consider the example of author Grace Paley's doctor:

> My abortion was a very clean and decent affair, but I didn't know until I got there that it would be alright. . . . The doctor had two or three rooms. My husband sat and waited in one of them. There were other people waiting for other kinds of care, which is how this doctor did it; he did a whole bunch of things. . . .
>
> The nurse was there during the procedure. He didn't give me an anesthetic; he said, 'If you want it, I'll give it to you, but it will be much safer and better if I don't.' It hurt, but it wasn't that painful. So I don't have anything traumatic to say about it. I was angry that I had to become a surreptitious person and that I was in danger, but the guy was very clean, and he was very good, and he was arrested within the next year. He went to jail.[5]

Abortion became a wedge that eroded the trust that many patients had previously felt for their doctors, as one woman recalls who had an illegal abortion with her physician's knowledge:

> I went [from New York] to Miami alone. When I got off the plane, I rented a car and drove to the address I had been given, which in fact was not the address where the doctor was, nor was it the address where the operation was going to be performed. They made

me wait there for hours to see if I had been followed. Then, they left my rented car at this address, put me in another car with two men who were Cuban and didn't speak English, and took me to another address. I had no idea where I was, where I was going, who I was with. . . .

I was very scared, and I think the only thing that kept me going was knowing what it would mean if I turned around and left. Where was I going to get better care? What was going to be different about the next place that I would go to? And the clock was ticking; you're only in your first couple of months for so long. . . .

The next day [after the abortion] I saw my doctor in New York, and he said they had done a very decent job. He knew I'd been pregnant because he was the one who told me, but he'd also told me there was nothing he could do. That was the hardest part of all. He felt badly that there was nothing he could do, and I certainly never quite felt the same toward him after that.[6]

Illegal abortion was exceedingly dangerous—and not only because some of the abortionists were greedy, incompetent, or cruel. There were additional, medically unacceptable, inherent hazards even if the person performing the procedure was well-meaning: inadequate facilities with no hospital backup, no regulation of training, no open scientific research in techniques and complications, lack of appropriate anesthesia, and so forth. Furthermore, the hostile legal climate surrounding abortion permeated other medical care for women, endangering their health. Grace Paley recalls the experience of a friend of hers who had not had an abortion. She was bleeding from her uterus, and it didn't stop:

> She went to the emergency room here at a Catholic hospital, and they refused to take care of her. They just flatly refused. They said she had to have a rabbit test to see if she was pregnant, and the results would take a couple of days. They would not touch her because she *might* be pregnant, and they *might* disturb the child. She continued to bleed, and they would not take care of her. She was a little skinny woman; she didn't have that much blood. Well, she wasn't pregnant. It turned out she had a tumor. It was an emergency—she had to be operated on immediately.
>
> Your life, a woman's life, was simply not the first thing that they had on their minds at all. Not only that: Even if the doctor had compassion—and in my friend's case, one of the doctors was very anxious about her—they couldn't do anything unless they were willing to risk a great deal.
>
> I think women died all the time when abortions were illegal. The horrible abortions were one way; the other way was the refusal of institutions—medical, church, and state— to care for you, their willingness to let you die.[7]

Support for Legalization. By the late 1960s, many Americans, for diverse reasons, supported making abortion legal under at least some circumstances. Physicians, lawyers, and even mainstream churches protested the inhumanity of compelling women to bear children if the children were likely to be deformed or if the women were in intolerable circumstances. And feminists in the new women's movement believed that women had a right to control their own bodies—a right that many of them felt should include access to abortion.

Some women decided to take the matter of abortion into their own hands. In Chicago, a group of women formed what they called the Jane Collective—a network that provided medically safe illegal abortions. When the women learned that one of their abortionists wasn't actually a doctor, they decided that they, too, though they were medical laywomen, could learn how to perform abortions safely. And so they did. The Jane Collective provided thousands of illegal abortions, and their competition put many of Chicago's dangerous and expensive illegal abortionists out of business.[8]

Across the nation it was state laws, not federal laws, that made abortion illegal. Slowly, these laws began to change. On the eve of *Roe* v. *Wade* (1973), the watershed Supreme Court case on abortion, only three states (Louisiana, New Hampshire, and Pennsylvania) absolutely prohibited abortion in all circumstances. Thirty-one states had more liberal laws that allowed abortions only to save the pregnant woman's life. Thirteen states allowed abortion under certain specific circumstances (typically danger to the woman's health, a likely deformed fetus, or pregnancy resulting from rape or incest), if the abortion was approved by doctors. And four states (Alaska, Washington, New York, and Hawaii) permitted abortions for any reason if performed before the fetus was able to survive outside the womb or before a specified term of pregnancy—between twenty and twenty-six weeks.[9]

In addition, in the decade before *Roe,* a legal foundation was laid in the United States Supreme Court for challenging the constitutionality of restrictive state abortion laws.

In 1965, in *Griswold* v. *Connecticut,* the Supreme Court struck down a state statute that outlawed the use of contraceptives on the grounds that the statute intruded into a constitutionally protected "zone of privacy" surrounding marital sexual relations. Writing for the Court's majority, Justice William O. Douglas asserted: "We deal with a right of privacy older than the Bill of Rights. . . . Would we allow the police to search the sacred precincts of marital bedrooms for tell-tale signs of the use of contraceptives? The very idea is repulsive to the notions of privacy surrounding the marriage relationship." [10]

Several years later, in *Eisenstadt* v. *Baird* (1972), the Court extended the *Griswold* ruling on the right of privacy to include unmarried individuals, concluding that there was no constitutional basis for treating unmarried citizens differently than married ones with regard to contraception:

> The marital couple is not an independent entity with a mind and heart of its own, but an *association of two individuals* each with a separate intellectual and emotional makeup. If the right to privacy means anything, it is the right of the individual, married or single, to be free from unwarranted governmental intrusion into matters so fundamentally affecting a person as the decision whether to bear or beget a child. [11]

In *Roe* v. *Wade,* the Court would apply this same logic to abortion.

3

Since
Roe *v.* Wade

In 1969, Norma McCorvey, a twenty-one-year-old Texas mother of a five-year-old daughter, single and mired in poverty, was pregnant again. She believed that in her circumstances having an abortion was the right thing to do—even though state law decreed that the abortion she sought was illegal.

Sarah Weddington and Linda Coffee, two young lawyers, believed that the law was wrong. McCorvey agreed to allow Weddington and Coffee to file a class-action suit against the state of Texas, on behalf of McCorvey and "others similarly situated," seeking for all women the legal right to choose abortion. Although the lawsuit would take too long to benefit her personally (she gave birth and gave up the child for adoption), McCorvey hoped that it would benefit other women.

District Attorney Henry Wade represented the state of Texas in this case. McCorvey, who was permitted to remain anonymous, became "Jane Roe" for purposes of the lawsuit. Their names, linked together as the lawsuit went through the federal court system, became synonymous with U.S. law on abortion when the Supreme Court ruled on their case, *Roe* v. *Wade,* in 1973.

Norma McCorvey was the plaintiff Jane Roe in the 1973 Supreme Court case Roe v. Wade, *in which Justice Harry Blackmun ruled that the government may not deny a woman the right to an abortion. McCorvey is celebrating Louisiana's veto of an anti-abortion bill in 1990.*

Writing for the Supreme Court's majority, Justice Harry Blackmun affirmed that "the 14th Amendment's concept of personal liberty" includes a "right to privacy," and he asserted that this right "is broad enough to encompass a woman's decision whether or not to terminate her pregnancy." Government thus may not deny women the right to have an abortion. The Court did not consider this right to be absolute, however. Instead, it concluded that certain "compelling" interests allowed the state to impinge upon women's right to privacy where abortion was concerned.[1]

One such interest was protecting women's health. This interest, the Court found, was sufficiently "compelling" to justify the state's becoming involved in abortion only when the medical risks of abortion become more dangerous to the woman's health than the risks of carrying the pregnancy to term—at about the end of the first trimester (first three months) of pregnancy. At that point, the state may begin to impose limitations or regulations on abortion—but only to protect women's health.

Another of the state's interests—protecting the life of the fetus—becomes sufficiently compelling, the court found, when the fetus becomes "viable," sufficiently developed to survive outside the womb. From that point forward, the state may flatly outlaw abortion in order to protect the life of the fetus, except when the life or health of the mother is endangered. (Viability, the Court later clarified, "must be a matter for the judgment of the responsible attending physician."[2])

Moral Versus Legal Issues. *Roe* v. *Wade* legalized abortion, effectively overturning all the laws prohibiting abortion on the books in states across the nation. It did not, however, resolve the debate about whether abortion is *morally* acceptable. If anything, *Roe*'s reasoning has obscured and made more difficult the moral issues relevant to abortion.

For example, viability is a fairly clear and consistent *legal* standard: A developing fetus becomes "viable" about the beginning of the third trimester of pregnancy. This biomedical reality hasn't changed substantially in the years since the *Roe* decision, nor does it seem likely to shift with changes in medical science in the foreseeable future. As a *moral* standard, however—as a guide to whether and when abortion is morally right—"viability" in the third trimester is murky. From a prospective mother's point of view, a healthy fetus is viable once it is safely implanted in her womb, because it will likely grow and thrive and eventually live independently of its mother—if she chooses to carry it to term. A pregnant woman's moral responsibilities have little to do with what medical science is capable of doing with a fetus outside the womb.

Roe's reasoning was concerned with privacy rather than with equality. Some people have made an "equality" argument that laws restricting abortion discriminate against women and violate the U.S. Constitution's requirement of equal protection under the law. The Supreme Court in the past has rejected such equality claims concerning other laws affecting pregnant women. Instead, the Supreme Court in *Roe* relied on the idea that each of us is legally entitled to privacy—the right to mind our own private affairs free of unreasonable government interference.

The problem with the privacy approach, as applied to abortion, is that it sidesteps the issue of individuals' responsibilities to others. As a result, Americans have not found common ground and reached consensus on this tough issue. Ruth Colker, a feminist legal scholar explains:

Feminist pro-choice litigators attempt to argue that we should consider the woman's right to autonomy in isolation from the state's interest in protecting life. Instead of seeing pregnant women as having an implicit connectedness to the fetus, and thus a responsibility to the well-being of that fetus, pregnant women are described in isolation from that fetus. Pro-life advocates do no better. . . . They try to remove fetuses from women's bodies and pretend that we can protect fetal life without controlling women's lives. Their concern for the autonomy or well-being of fetuses causes them to disregard women's lives.[3]

"Privacy" alone does not reconcile the rights and interests of a pregnant woman with those of her developing fetus, her husband, or her parents, or even with those of society at large.

***Legal Issues Since* Roe.** The Supreme Court since *Roe* v. *Wade* has heard more than a dozen major cases concerning abortion.

These cases have focused on several key issues: husband's consent, parental consent for young girls, public funding for abortion, and permissible state restrictions under the *Roe* ruling.

HUSBAND'S CONSENT. The Supreme Court, in *Danforth* v. *Planned Parenthood of Missouri* (1976), decreed that states may not require a woman to obtain her husband's consent before undergoing an abortion. Writing for the majority, Justice Blackmun observed that it's best that

Associate Justice Harry Blackmun wrote
in 1974 that the abortion decision "will be
regarded as one of the first worst mistakes
in the Court's history or one of its great
decisions, a turning point."

partners agree on such a decision. If, however, they do
disagree about whether to have an abortion, then the
woman should prevail because "it is the woman who
physically bears the child and who is directly and more
immediately affected by the pregnancy."[4] The decision
does not deal explicitly with unmarried couples, but as
a practical matter the law on this issue seems to be
settled.

PARENTAL CONSENT. The right of parents to decide whether or not their minor child may have an abortion is a more complicated and less settled issue. Most minors who have abortions do so with a parent's knowledge, and most parents support the decision to have an abortion. Since *Roe,* however, the Supreme Court has held that a child capable of making a mature and informed decision has a right to decide to have an abortion whether her parents consent to it or not, at least in the early stages of pregnancy, when the physical risks of an abortion are less than those for carrying the pregnancy to full term.[5] Furthermore, the state may not even require the child to *notify* her parents unless it also sets up a reasonable and accessible procedure for the child to obtain a judge's approval for going ahead with an early abortion without notifying her parents.[6] Going before a judge to ask permission for an abortion can be a difficult experience, more difficult than the abortion itself, as one young woman who went through it recalls:

> I was sixteen, pregnant and couldn't tell my parents. It's not that they would hurt me or anything like that—but I didn't want to hurt them. Because I wasn't getting my parents' permission, I had to go in front of a judge. I felt like a criminal. I was scared that he would say no. My lawyer helped a lot, but it was still so hard to do. It made me angry, too. This judge doesn't even know me. Even though he let me do what I wanted to do—have an abortion—I'm still mad about the judge. The abortion itself was fine. I feel good that I was able to do all of this.[7]

About half the states have enacted laws requiring minors seeking abortions to notify parents. Many pro-choice activists contend that these laws cause many pregnant teenagers not to avoid abortions but to have them later in pregnancy (after they've gotten past the notification hurdle one way or another), when abortions are more difficult and dangerous. Anti-abortion activists, on the other hand, contend that many pregnant teenagers who are too immature to make truly informed decisions about abortion have suffered serious medical complications from having had abortions that their parents would have refused to allow.

A child's right to privacy is not absolute. In the past, the law has given parents complete authority over their children, and it is only in the past few decades that U.S. law has been willing to enforce the rights of children in some limited cases when they conflict with the authority of their parents. Early abortion is such a case. The law still generally recognizes and enforces parents' rights to be informed about and to grant or withhold consent for medical procedures—including abortion—performed on their children. The law also, however, recognizes a pregnant girl's right, as defined in the *Roe* case, to decide privately, in consultation with her doctor, to have an abortion. The Supreme Court has held that if the girl is mature enough to make such an informed decision, then her right to choose abortion privately outweighs her parents' right to grant or withhold consent.

PUBLIC FUNDING AND FACILITIES. In two 1977 cases, the Supreme Court held that states have to pay only for "necessary" or "therapeutic" abortions as part of the package of health services the state makes available to poor women.[8] In another case that same year, the Court ruled that public hospitals (which provide much of poor women's medical care) are not required to provide elective abortions, even if they provide childbirth services.[9]

In these decisions, the Court reasoned that the policies in question did not impinge upon women's fundamental right to choose abortion, only upon who would pay for the procedure and where it would be available. Furthermore, it found that the state may promote childbirth by paying for it while refusing to pay for elective abortions. Justice William Brennan, dissenting, contended that "this disparity in funding by the State clearly operates to coerce indigent pregnant women to bear children they would not otherwise choose to have."[10]

These 1977 decisions pertained only to the laws of particular states. Other states were free to follow less restrictive funding policies. In 1980, however, the Court made a much further-reaching decision when it upheld the constitutionality of the Hyde amendment.

The Hyde amendment, sponsored by Representative Henry Hyde of Illinois, was first passed by Congress in 1976, then immediately challenged in court. It cuts off federal funding for nearly all abortions. (Before Hyde, about one third of all abortions were funded by Medicaid.[11]) The Hyde amendment has had the support not only of those who are opposed to the legalization of abortion, but also of many who support a legal right to choose but are nonetheless uncomfortable with public funding for "abortion on demand." President Jimmy Carter, for example, during his four-year term in office in the late 1970s, noted that "there are many things in life that are not fair, that wealthy people can afford and poor people can't. But I don't believe that the federal government should take action to try to make these opportunities exactly equal, particularly when there is a moral factor involved."[12]

When the Supreme Court finally decided, in 1980 in *Harris* v. *McCrae,* that the Hyde amendment was permitted by the U.S. Constitution, the amendment read:

None of the funds provided by this joint resolution [of Congress] shall be used to perform
abortions except where the life of the mother
would be endangered if the fetus were carried
to term; or except for such medical procedures
necessary for the victims of rape or incest
when such rape or incest has been reported
promptly to a law enforcement agency or public health service.[13]

Writing for the Supreme Court's majority, Justice Potter
Stewart not only declared the Hyde amendment constitutional, but also indicated how and why the state might
legitimately encourage women to have babies rather
than abortions:

By subsidizing the medical expenses of indigent women who carry their pregnancies to
term while not subsidizing the comparable expenses of women who undergo abortions (except those whose lives are threatened) Congress has established incentives that make
childbirth a more attractive alternative than
abortion for persons eligible for Medicaid.
These incentives bear a direct relationship to
the legitimate congressional interest in protecting potential life.[14]

Because federal funds are used in all the states' Medicaid programs, the Hyde amendment has had the effect
of eliminating public funding not only for all elective
abortions but also for many therapeutic abortions (those
intended to end pregnancies that endanger the health but
not necessarily the life of the pregnant woman). In
1992, only 13 percent of abortions performed in the
United States were paid for with public funding, with

virtually all of the money coming from state governments. About a dozen states in the early 1990s were using their own funds to pay for abortions for low-income women.[15]

While restrictions on public funding for abortion have likely created financial hardships for them, many poor women nonetheless have continued to have abortions. One study, for example, published in 1984, concluded that lack of funding didn't deny poor women abortions, but it delayed their getting them by an average of two to three weeks.[16]

RESTRICTIONS. In the years after *Roe*, various state legislatures and local governments crafted dozens of laws intended to restrict abortion that fit legally within *Roe*'s requirements. Some of these laws' restrictions have been upheld, among them that women may be required by the state to give written, informed consent and that physicians may be required to keep records on all abortions if the records are kept confidential and serve the interests of maternal health.[17]

The Supreme Court has struck down proposed restrictions requiring that two physicians must approve an abortion before it can be performed;[18] that physicians must try to save the life of a not-yet-viable aborted fetus;[19] and that all abortions after the first trimester must be performed in a hospital, rather than a clinic or doctor's office, where the procedure is in most cases safe and much less expensive.[20]

In the future, if the Supreme Court shifts its position to allow more restrictions on abortion, these are the sorts of restrictions that state legislatures will likely once again seek to impose.

In 1986, the Supreme Court explicitly and sweepingly reaffirmed that the position it had taken in the *Roe* decision remained the law of the land. In the majority opinion for *Thornburgh* v. *ACOG,* a decision that struck down a half dozen provisions in a Pennsylvania law restricting abortion, Justice Blackmun wrote:

> Again today, we affirm the general principles laid down in *Roe.* . . . In the years since this Court's decision in *Roe* states and municipalities have adopted a number of measures seemingly designed to prevent a woman from exercising freedom of choice. . . . But the constitutional principles that led this Court to its decisions in 1973 still provide the compelling reason for recognizing the constitutional dimensions of a woman's right to decide whether to end her pregnancy. 'It should go without saying that the vitality of these constitutional principles cannot be allowed to yield simply because of disagreement with them.' . . . The States are not free, under the guise of protecting maternal health or fetal life, to intimidate women into continuing pregnancies.[21]

Then, on July 3, 1989, the Supreme Court announced its decision in *Webster* v. *Reproductive Health Services.* Although the Court stopped short of overruling *Roe,* it nonetheless decreed that the Missouri anti-abortion statute challenged in *Webster* was constitutional. That statute decreed that human life begins at conception; prohibited use of state-funded facilities or employees for abortion services; and required that doctors test for fetal viability for abortions scheduled for twenty weeks after conception or later. Furthermore, the Court indicated that it was willing to hear additional cases intended to test *Roe* further.

Norma McCorvey and her lawyer Gloria Allred outside the Supreme Court with demonstrators while the Court listens to opening arguments in Webster v. Reproductive Health Services. *In its ruling on this 1989 case, the Court fell one vote short of overturning* Roe v. Wade.

The *Webster* case made clear that the Supreme Court was deeply divided on the abortion issue. Only a narrow majority of five out of the nine justices (two who had originally opposed *Roe,* plus the three justices appointed by President Ronald Reagan, a vocal opponent of abortion) favored the majority decision carefully and narrowly crafted by Chief Justice William Rehnquist. And two of those five wrote concurring opinions that spelled out serious concerns they had about the majority decision.

Justice Blackmun, who had written the Court's opinion for *Roe,* bitterly criticized the *Webster* decision. In his dissenting opinion he spelled out his fear that the Court was set upon destroying *Roe* "not with a bang, but a whimper." He concluded: "For today, at least, the law of abortion stands undisturbed. For today, at least, the women of this nation still retain the liberty to control their destinies. But the signs are evident and very ominous, and a chill wind blows. I dissent." [22]

SINCE *WEBSTER.* In June 1990 the Court ruled on two similar cases concerning parental notification: *Hodgson* v. *Minnesota* and *Ohio* v. *Akron Center for Reproductive Health.* The Minnesota law in question in *Hodgson* required a minor seeking an abortion to notify but not necessarily obtain the permission of both her parents; the *Ohio* statute required minors to notify at least one parent. The Court held, unsurprisingly, that such notification requirements were constitutional only as long as each girl had the option of going before a judge for permission to proceed without notifying her parents.

In 1991, in the case of *Rust* v. *Sullivan,* the Supreme Court upheld the so-called gag rule, a federal directive prohibiting doctors and counselors working at family-planning facilities that receive federal funding from providing information about abortion or referring patients to abortion providers.

In 1992, the Supreme Court further signaled its willingness to allow state laws to make it more difficult for women to obtain abortions. *Planned Parenthood* v. *Casey* clearly affirmed the legal right to choose abortion. Nonetheless, by a narrow 5–4 margin, the Court upheld various restrictions on abortion imposed by a Pennsylvania law—even though those restrictions were found to be burdensome and medically unnecessary. The Court agreed that Pennsylvania could require physicians to give counseling favoring childbirth to all women seeking abortions, could require a twenty-four-hour waiting period before an abortion could be performed, and could require parental notification. (The Court did strike down the law's "unduly burdensome" requirement that women notify their husbands before undergoing an abortion.)

Thus, as of late 1995, *Roe* v. *Wade* remained by and large the law of the land on abortion, although the Supreme Court had in prior years allowed federal regulations and state laws to nibble away at access to abortion. Since *Webster,* especially, legislation restricting abortion has been proposed and debated in state legislatures across the country. Most of these bills have not become law, however, and most states' laws have remained essentially pro-choice.

4

The Medical Picture

In the years since *Roe* v. *Wade,* not only have most of the unsafe, illegal abortionists been put out of business but also *legal* abortion has become much safer. In 1973, the risk of death from having a legal abortion was 3.4 deaths per 100,000 abortions. By 1987, the risk of death was only 0.4 per 100,000.[1]

Although a great deal has changed since abortion was legalized, in some respects abortion continues to be poorly integrated into the U.S. health-care system. Some private health-insurance plans cover abortion procedures, some don't. (Most public funding for elective abortion has long been forbidden by the Hyde amendment and various state laws.) And many doctors and health facilities don't perform abortions.

Availability of Abortion. A woman considering abortion needs appropriate medical care, and she needs it quickly. Ideally, she would go to her regular family physician or gynecologist, who would determine whether or not she is in fact pregnant, explain to her various choices she may elect (carrying the pregnancy to term as well as options for abortion) and how they fit with her personal medical history, help her to reach a decision, then provide prenatal care or abortion services, either in the doctor's office or at a clinic or hospital with which the practitioner is affiliated.

In the United States in the 1990s, however, this scenario is unusual. Many women don't have a family physician, others feel uncomfortable discussing abortion with their regular doctors, and some doctors are uncomfortable discussing abortion with their patients. Many obstetricians and gynecologists (doctors who specialize in women's reproductive health) refuse to perform abortions, and others will perform them only in limited circumstances. Some doctors are morally opposed to abortion; other are reluctant to provide abortions to their patients because they do not want to become targets for anti-abortion protests.

Some doctors who used to perform abortions have stopped doing so because they have developed moral qualms about the procedure. In the 1960s, Bernard Nathanson, an obstetrician/gynecologist, was a leader in the movement to liberalize the nation's abortion laws and a cofounder of the National Association for the Repeal of Abortion Laws, the organization that later became the National Abortion Rights Action League (NARAL). (It now calls itself the National Abortion and Reproductive Rights Action League.) Nathanson believed that safe, legal abortions should be available to all women who sought them. By 1976, though, his beliefs had changed. "One day, I cannot now recall the patient or the circumstances, I decided that I would perform no more of the grotesque 'second trimester' abortions except on strict medical grounds—even for long-time patients in my private practice. Around the same time I also began refusing to do elective abortions at *any* stage for new patients who came to me. And so quietly, without fanfare or notice, I was out of the elective abortion business."[2] By the 1980s, Nathanson had become a prominent *anti*-abortion activist.

Many obstetricians and gynecologists have no experience with abortion procedures, and few primary-care physicians today perform abortions. The number of medical schools offering abortion training to their obstetrics residents has dropped in recent years; as of 1992, one third of all U.S. medical schools offered no training in abortion.[3]

Most U.S. abortions, especially early abortions, are thus now performed by specialists, often at clinics solely devoted to reproductive health services. (More than 90 percent of all abortions are performed in clinics or doctors' offices, rather than in hospitals.[4]) A woman seeking an abortion may find such a clinic on her own, or she may be referred to one by her regular physician. Although clinics that provide abortions often also provide a variety of women's health services, they are widely perceived as "abortion clinics" and are the particular targets of anti-abortion protest.

The shrinking number of doctors trained in abortion procedures and willing to perform them, the growing aggressiveness of anti-abortion protest, and other causes have reduced the number of places where abortion services are provided. Since the early 1980s, more than 500 hospitals and clinics have stopped providing abortions.[5] According to the Alan Guttmacher Institute, "84 percent of all U.S. counties lacked an abortion provider in 1992, yet these counties were home to 30 percent of all women aged 15–44."[6] Smaller towns and rural areas in the Midwest and the South have become especially underserviced.

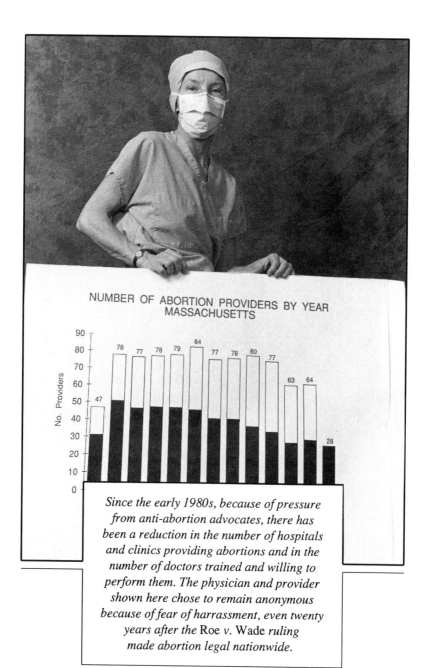

NUMBER OF ABORTION PROVIDERS BY YEAR
MASSACHUSETTS

Since the early 1980s, because of pressure
from anti-abortion advocates, there has
been a reduction in the number of hospitals
and clinics providing abortions and in the
number of doctors trained and willing to
perform them. The physician and provider
shown here chose to remain anonymous
because of fear of harrassment, even twenty
years after the Roe v. Wade ruling
made abortion legal nationwide.

Social Conditions. The medical risks and implications of abortion—and of carrying a pregnancy to term—are greatly affected by the economic and social conditions of individual women and by the way in which health care is or is not delivered to them.[7]

Early abortions are both monetarily cheaper and less medically risky than childbirth, even for women who have good medical care. However, medical care generally and good prenatal care especially are not readily available to many women, particularly teenagers and working women who aren't covered by Medicaid and can't afford private health insurance. Inadequate prenatal care greatly increases the risks associated with giving birth, both for the mother and for the baby.

Teenagers who give birth are more likely to suffer serious medical complications—from miscarriage to premature delivery to hemorrhage to death—than older mothers. Much of this difference seems to be due to poverty and inadequate health care rather than simply to youth.

The socioeconomic effects of early childbirth also clearly have long-term implications for maternal and child health. Teenage mothers are less likely to graduate from high school and less likely to do well economically than young women who give birth later, and these disadvantages tend to translate into poorer health and development for both mother and child.

Babies born to teenage mothers are more likely to have low birth weights and to experience other problems at birth, and this correlation seems to be due to socioeconomic rather than biological factors. As children of adolescent mothers grow up, however, they tend to do more poorly than children of older mothers—they lag in learning and social development, tend to have more illnesses and accidents, and so on—and this effect ap-

WHO HAS ABORTIONS AND WHY?

One of the best sources of clear and accurate information about abortion in the United States is the Alan Guttmacher Institute, a nonprofit organization that performs reproductive health research, policy analysis, and public education. According to the institute:

- More than 50 percent of the pregnancies among American women are unintended—half of these are terminated by abortion.
- In 1992, there were 1.5 million abortions in the United States.
- Each year nearly 3 out of 100 women aged 15–44 have an abortion.
- Of women obtaining abortions, 56 percent are under age 25, including 23 percent who are teenagers; only 22 percent are over 30.
- In 1992, 406,000 [abortions] were obtained by teenagers.
- Only 9 percent of women having abortions have never used birth control; [but], more than one quarter of unmarried teenagers under the age of 18 who get abortions have never used birth control.
- Unmarried women are five times more likely than married women to have an abortion.
- Poor women are about three times more likely to have abortions. Nevertheless, 11 percent of abortions are obtained by women whose household incomes are $50,000 or more.
- While white women account for 65 percent of all abortions, the nonwhite abortion rate is more than twice the white rate (57 versus 21 per 1,000).
- About 70 percent of women who have an abortion say that they intend to have children in the future.
- On average, women report more than three reasons that lead them to choose abortion: three quarters say that having a baby would interfere with work, school, or other responsibilities; about two thirds say they can't afford to have a child; one half say they do not want to be a single parent or have problems in their relationships with their partners.
- Of teenagers having abortions, three quarters say they cannot afford to have a baby, and two thirds think they are not mature enough.
- Of women having abortions, 1 percent have been advised that the fetus has a defect, and an additional 12 percent fear that the fetus may have been harmed by medications or other conditions.
- About 16,000 women have abortions each year because they become pregnant as a result of rape or incest.[8]

pears not to be entirely due to poverty and other socio-economic factors.

Society's restrictions on abortion (including the parental notification requirements and other restrictions enacted by state legislatures in recent years) have additional medical implications. Making abortions more difficult to obtain doesn't alter the risks of giving birth, and it appears to have little effect on the number of abortions ultimately performed. Obstacles to access do, however, *delay* abortions, so that many women (especially poorer, younger women for whom the obstacles are most formidable) end up having abortions later in pregnancy, when both the medical risks and the financial costs are higher.

Before an Abortion Is Performed. A woman considering abortion must first make sure that she is pregnant. Pregnancy tests (available over-the-counter in drugstores, as well as in doctors' offices and clinics) can reliably detect pregnancy shortly after a pregnant woman's first missed menstrual period.

Once a woman is sure that she's pregnant, she must have medical examinations to determine how far her pregnancy has progressed and whether factors in her medical history create or increase special risks associated with particular abortion procedures or with carrying her pregnancy to term. Each pregnant woman is routinely tested for Rh factor. (If her blood is Rh negative, a genetic trait, she'll need to receive a special injection after abortion or childbirth to prevent complications with future pregnancies.) Many abortion providers also routinely test for sexually transmitted diseases (STD) and may require women who are infected to be treated before proceeding with an abortion, in order to avoid possibly spreading the infection into the upper part of the reproductive system.

Medical ethics require that each patient understand the risks and benefits of all of her options and freely choose to go ahead with the option she decides upon. This is called "informed consent," and patients about to undergo abortion are routinely counseled and then required to sign forms attesting that they understand and consent to the procedure. In many states, the requirements spelled out in state law for informed consent for abortion go well beyond the consent requirements for other medical procedures.

First-Trimester Abortions. If a woman has had unprotected sexual intercourse at a time during her menstrual cycle when she's most likely to become pregnant, and if this was an isolated incident and no more than seventy-two hours has passed since it occurred, she may be a good candidate for a "morning-after pill." This pill, a powerful dose of hormones that must be administered under a doctor's supervision, prevents any embryo from attaching itself to the wall of the woman's uterus and thus prevents pregnancy from proceeding. Because the morning-after pill acts before implantation takes place— as does, for example, birth control by an intrauterine device (IUD)—use of it is not considered an abortion. It is of special value for rape victims, and for women whose usual means of birth control has suddenly failed, as when a condom breaks or a diaphragm slips. Instead of a morning-after pill, some women choose to have an IUD inserted, which will both immediately prevent implantation from occurring and provide ongoing birth control.

Abortion properly refers to pregnancies ended after implantation has occurred, usually about one week after conception. Most abortions—89 percent—take place early in pregnancy, during the first trimester, when the procedures are much safer and medically simpler, and most of these take place in the first eight weeks of pregnancy.[9]

Since the early 1980s, a pill called RU-486 has been widely used to induce early abortions in Europe—but not in the United States. Its manufacturer, reluctant to incite the wrath of anti-abortion protesters, for years avoided marketing the pill in the United States. In 1994, it made U.S. patent rights for the pill available to a non-profit organization that intended to bring the pill to the U.S. market in 1996.

RU-486 works rather like a morning-after pill, but it's powerful enough to end a pregnancy even after implantation has occurred. Although complications do sometimes occur with RU-486, it appears to be less risky overall than surgical abortion for patients in the first two months of pregnancy. RU-486 isn't perfect. It takes longer than an early surgical abortion, it requires several visits to a doctor's office or clinic, and a significant number of patients who use it end up needing surgical treatment anyway.

In mid-1995, researchers announced a readily available alternative to RU-486. Two other drugs, methotrexate and misprostol, taken in succession under a doctor's supervision, could safely be used to cause abortion in the first nine weeks of pregnancy. Unlike RU-486, these two drugs were already widely available in the United States because they had been approved by the federal Food and Drug Administration for other medical purposes.[10]

The currently preferred surgical method for first-trimester abortion is vacuum aspiration. To perform this procedure, the physician usually first dilates the patient's cervix (expands the opening from the vagina to the uterus by inserting a slim rod or similar device). More advanced pregnancies generally require greater dilation, since more tissue must be removed from the uterus. Next, a sterile strawlike tube attached to a vacuuming device is inserted into the uterus, and the physician suctions out the contents of the uterus: embryo or fetus, placenta, and the lining of the uterus thickened by pregnancy. It is very important to remove all of the contents of the uterus, and the physician may use a metal loop called a curette to scrape the walls of the uterus to ensure that bits of tissue don't remain behind.

Vacuum aspiration is usually done in a doctor's office or clinic rather than in a hospital, and it is usually done under local anesthesia of the cervix. Some cramping is usual, as the uterus responds to manipulation of the cervix and then shrinks to its non-pregnant size during and after the procedure. Most women find vacuum aspiration, which typically takes five to fifteen minutes, uncomfortable but not unbearable. Many experience cramping and discomfort similar to having an IUD inserted; some experience severe pain and prolonged cramping; a few report little discomfort at all.

The medical risks associated with vacuum-aspiration abortion in the first trimester are low—significantly lower than the medical risks of carrying a pregnancy to term. Uncomplicated first-trimester vacuum-aspiration abortions do not appear to cause problems with later childbearing. Sometimes, though very rarely, serious medical complications do occur after these abortions, including excessive bleeding (typically caused by fetal or placental tissue left in the uterus after the procedure) and infection.

Later Abortions. After the third month of pregnancy, simple vacuum aspiration is no longer feasible. Abortions become riskier with each passing week—more dangerous, more complicated, and more expensive. Nonetheless, thousands of women do have second-trimester abortions each year. (Abortion in the third trimester of pregnancy, by which time the fetus is capable or nearly capable of surviving outside the womb, is not performed except in rare cases in which the mother's life is endangered by continuing the pregnancy. Only about 100 to 200 third-trimester abortions take place each year in the United States.[11])

The most common reasons for delaying abortion past the first trimester are personal or practical rather than medical. According to the Guttmacher Institute, "Most women who have an abortion after 15 weeks of pregnancy have had problems detecting their pregnancy."[12] Some women deny their pregnancy, or have difficulty deciding what to do. And many women, denied public funding for abortion, find it takes them a long time to come up with several hundred dollars to pay for the procedure.

A small number of women abort in the second trimester because their fetuses are or may be badly damaged or deformed. Some may have been exposed to diseases or toxic substances strongly associated with birth defects. Others (and this is the more common scenario) have undergone a test called amniocentesis and received results indicating a fetus with Down syndrome, a spinal disorder, or some other severe congenital defect. Amniocentesis cannot be performed before the fourth month of pregnancy; by the time the results of the test are available, women who have undergone it are well into the second trimester. According to one woman who decided to abort a fetus with Down syndrome, "The psychological pain is enormous. Deciding to end the life of a fetus you've wanted and carried for most of five months is no easy matter. The number of relatively late second-trimester abortions performed for genetic reasons is very small. It seems an almost inconsequential number, unless you happen to be one of them." [13]

Dilation and evacuation (D&E) is the currently preferred method for most second-trimester abortions. It is similar to vacuum aspiration, but because there is now more fetal and placental tissue in the uterus, and the uterus is larger and softer and more easily damaged, the procedure takes longer and is more difficult. It is usually performed in a hospital, rather than in a doctor's office or clinic, and most patients are given more extensive anesthesia than for first-trimester abortions. Once the patient's cervix has been dilated (wider than is required for earlier abortions), the physician removes pieces of fetal and placental tissue from the uterus with forceps, scrapes the walls of the uterus with a curette, and vacuums blood and tissue from the uterus. The procedure takes longer than vacuum aspiration (typically fifteen to forty-five minutes), and it carries an increased risk of the same sorts of complications, as well as some additional risks, including perforation of the uterus and tearing of the cervix.

D&E is not available everywhere. Many doctors have not taken the special training the procedure requires, or they dislike the idea of performing it, and they prefer "induction abortion," or "instillation abortion," for second-trimester patients. In an induction abortion, premature labor is induced by injecting saline solution (salty water) or a hormone directly into the sac that holds the fetus inside the woman's uterus. The woman's uterus contracts and expels the fetus and placenta, much as it would during a normal childbirth. An induction abortion, performed in a hospital, takes many hours to complete and is much more difficult for the woman than a D&E. Risks of complications with an in-

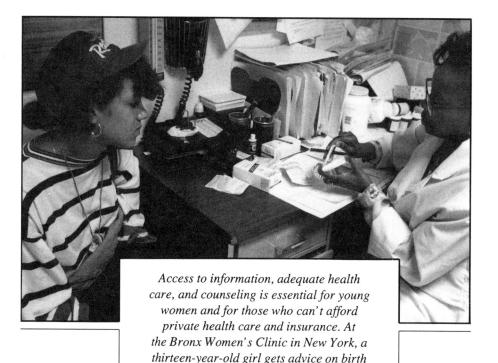

Access to information, adequate health care, and counseling is essential for young women and for those who can't afford private health care and insurance. At the Bronx Women's Clinic in New York, a thirteen-year-old girl gets advice on birth control methods and the prevention of HIV.

duction abortion are similar to those of carrying a pregnancy to term and much higher than with a D&E. As many as one quarter to one third of all induction abortions are "incomplete"—tissue remains behind in the uterus that must later be expelled or otherwise removed.[14]

Psychological Effects of Abortion. The long-range psychological effects of abortion have been hotly debated in recent years. Many anti-abortion activists assert that abortion is both morally and psychologically damaging to the women who undergo it.

Each woman's experience with abortion is unique, and the emotional and psychological aftermath of abortion varies a great deal from one woman to another. Some women describe complicated, changing mixtures of conflicting feelings about their abortions:

> After the abortion, the overpowering feeling was one of such relief: You thought, It's over, and you're still here. But the next day, you can get depressed as hell. I think the hormonal turnaround is a great part of it. . . .
>
> I will add that I never felt the fetus was a person. I didn't then; I don't now. But naturally, you do think of the person who might have been.
>
> You could briefly cheer yourself up by thinking of the worst characteristics in both your families, but still, you do have the sense of the loss of a potential person.[15]

Not everyone, however, reports being depressed after having an abortion:

> I was nervous about the abortion. If you've got to go and have surgery, you're scared. The nurse said to me, 'People have all kinds of reactions to abortion. Some cry . . . they're real upset when it's over.' Well, when mine was over, I was hysterical with laughter. I just couldn't stop laughing. I think it was anxiety. You know how you yawn when you're anxious? That was the form of relief for me . . . it was relief.[16]

Some women report post-abortion grief that lingers for years because they have found no way to acknowledge it openly and find peace. One woman recalls:

I had an abortion when I was seventeen. It was illegal then, so my parents took me to Mexico. The memories were painful. But I never talked about them.

When I was twenty-two I had an abortion, part of the ending of a marriage. It was still illegal in Arizona, so I went to California. . . .

At age twenty-six a second marriage ended with my third abortion. It was now legal in Arizona, so I didn't have to run away. It was neat, clean, and fast. I woke from the anesthetic sobbing. The nurse, trying to comfort me, repeated, 'It's all right, dear. It's over. It's over.' I knew—that's why I cried. But I didn't talk about it.

The American Psychological Association announced recently that 'most women who have abortions experience a sense of relief,' rather than 'any lasting psychological trauma.' I felt that relief—every time.

I got on with my life, as everyone around me advised. . . .

For so many years—I resisted—thinking about the abortions. It always hurt too much. After the first one, I would count years by their ages. I'd imagine how old each child would have been that year. After the second, after the third, it became too difficult to carry their ages. I knew it was a hurting thing to do. I accepted the abortions as done, as choices,

Anti-abortion demonstrators and a pro-choice activist outside a Planned Parenthood clinic. The pro-choice volunteers protect women arriving at the clinic for abortions or counseling from harassment.

awful choices, between fire and ice, between rocks and hard places. . . .

I didn't have three abortions because I was a bad, but simply a hurting girl, alone and denying a part of myself I could not accept. No one told me that a woman, a girl, who chooses to end a pregnancy has the right to mourn. I thought that since I had *chosen* abortion, I had given up that right.[17]

Most abortion facilities provide post-abortion counseling for their patients. Outside the clinic, however, many women encounter a great deal of hostility to abortion and a shortage of support for working through the emotional, psychological, and spiritual ramifications of having had an abortion.

Encouraging women to come to peace with their abortions might encourage not only women's psychological health but also social consensus. Encouraging respect for life *and* compassion for the women who choose abortion *and* grief for the loss inherent in abortion might together help create common ground for the diverse moral perspectives on the abortion issue in the United States.

5

Moral Perspectives

There is no scientific consensus that a human life begins at conception, at a given stage of fetal development, or at birth. The question of 'when a human life begins' cannot be answered by reference to scientific principles. . . . The answer to that question will depend on each individual's social, religious, philosophical, ethical and moral beliefs and values.

Amicus brief submitted to the Supreme Court
in the *Webster* case, signed by
167 scientists, 11 of them Nobel laureates[1]

Mario Cuomo, three-term governor of New York and a practicing Catholic, during the 1980s and 1990s clashed repeatedly with conservative church leaders as he sought to reconcile his obligations as a Catholic with his duties as a public servant. He consistently and publicly stated that he accepted the church's teaching on abortion: that it is a grave sin. However, he argued, it would be wrong for an elected official in a democracy such as the

Although former New York governor Mario Cuomo does not personally support abortion, he supports its legality.

United States to insist that everyone accept his or her church's moral teachings. Furthermore, moral teachings ought not to be written into law unless they reflect a general public consensus about what's right and what's wrong. Cuomo reasoned that, since there is no such consensus on abortion in the United States today, abortion should not be made criminal. "Here in America," Cuomo wrote, "where the law permits women to have abortions and preserves their right not to have abortions, the terrible, hard judgment which that freedom permits must be a matter of the woman's conscience."[2]

New York Archbishop John J. O'Connor disagreed: "Where Catholics are perceived not only as treating church teaching on abortion with contempt, but helping to multiply abortions, by advocating legislation supporting abortion, or by making public funds available for abortion, bishops must decide that for the common good, such Catholics must be warned that they are at risk of excommunication. If such actions persist, bishops may consider excommunication the only option."[3]

Although O'Connor did not excommunicate Cuomo, excommunication (banishment from the church's central sacrament of holy communion) was not an idle threat. In July 1990 the director and one of the doctors at a Texas abortion clinic revealed that they had been excommunicated because, as their notices of excommunication read: "Your cooperation in producing abortions is a sin against God and humanity and against the law of the Roman Catholic Church."[4]

Religious Views on Abortion. The church has not always been so absolutely opposed to abortion. In its earliest days, Christianity followed the lead of Judaism in considering the fetus to have a life separate from that of its mother and deeming it appropriate to view and treat that life according to its stage of development. Early Christians seem to have viewed abortion as a sin, but not as a murder until the fetus was developed well beyond conception. The question of when the fetus became a person remained unsettled for centuries.[5]

In the thirteenth century Thomas Aquinas, a Catholic scholar whose work greatly shaped modern Catholic theology, wrote that the soul enters the body of the fetus and human life begins well after conception (at forty days for a male, eighty days for a female) and that prior to that point abortion is not a mortal sin (a sin for which one could be condemned to hell). In 1869, Pope Pius IX decreed that abortion at any point in pregnancy was an offense to be met with excommunication. Since then, the Catholic Church has been uncompromisingly anti-abortion. In a 1995 encyclical covering many life-and-death issues, Pope John Paul II reiterated the church's position that abortion is always sinful.[6]

Some Catholic theologians, however, have expressed doubts that the abortion issue is so clear-cut. For example, seeking a more direct understanding of abortion, David Maguire, a professor of moral theology at a Jesuit university, visited an abortion clinic in the mid-1980s. There he met a pregnant woman who was being treated for bipolar disorder with lithium, a drug that causes birth defects. She had decided to have an abortion. Maguire later wrote:

> As I watched this woman, I thought of one of my colleagues who had recently made a confident assertion that there could be no plausible reason for abortion except to save the physical life of the woman or if the fetus was anence-

phalic [lacking a brain]. This woman's physical life was not at risk and the embryo would develop a brain. But saving *life* involves more than cardiopulmonary continuity. How is it that in speaking of women we so easily reduce human life to physical life? What certitudes persuade theologians that there are only two marginal reasons to justify abortion? Why is the Vatican comparably sure that while there may be *just* wars with incredible slaughter, there can be no *just* abortions? Both need to listen to the woman on lithium as she testifies that life does not always confine itself within the ridges of our theories.[7]

Many feminists within the Catholic Church are uncomfortable with its positions on reproductive issues. Feminist nuns have called for an open-minded dialogue within the Church on abortion:

Every woman has a free will. God gave us free will . . . that's what separates us from the beasts. Free will is guided by conscience, and conscience is formed not only by dogma, what organized religions tell us, but by experience. A woman will answer to God for one thing: Has she followed her conscience in carrying out God's will? It's nobody's right to tell her what her conscience said to her. That's what men want to take from us . . . the right to follow our own conscience.[8]

Outside the Catholic Church, religious organizations have held diverse views on abortion, ranging from the long-held absolute opposition of Southern Baptists to unambiguous pro-choice advocacy. In the 1960s, approximately 1,500 ministers and rabbis all over the country who were concerned about the safety of women facing the terrible risks of illegal abortion operated the underground Clergy Consultation Service on Abortion. Risking imprisonment for their efforts, participating clergy helped women find doctors who were willing to give them abortions.[9] A cofounder of the service explains his religious motivations for participating:

> In my religious tradition, birth was never seen as anything but a gift, a miraculous, marvelous surprise present—a gift of God and a woman stranger. To speak of being born as a right is to jar the sensibilities and strain the moral syntax of existence. We are born of human intentions at the cost of real physical pain and the nourishing love of a woman which ought never be forced, compelled, or mandated by another person or the state.[10]

By the 1970s most mainstream Protestant churches publicly supported the legalization of abortion. In the 1980s, however, this picture changed. Many denominations—from Eastern Orthodox churches to Mormons to Lutherans, Baptists, and Episcopalians—came to oppose abortion entirely or to approve of it only in limited circumstances.

Religious opposition to abortion, from the conservative Catholic Church to the radical Operation Rescue organization, is grounded in a belief that abortion is literally murder, or at least so antithetical to life that it is unacceptable to God. According to the National Conference of Catholic Bishops, abortion is wrong because "it involves taking the life of an innocent, unborn human

The doctrines of some religious groups consider abortion an act of murder and therefore morally wrong. Operation Rescue, a radical Catholic organization, frequently stages demonstrations like this one, blocking entrances to abortion clinics.

being. The child in the womb is human in origin, destiny and make-up. This newly conceived child is one of us. Human life comes into being at conception, and from conception on each new human being possesses all that is internally required to grow and develop into a mature adult."[11]

Many anti-abortion activists have likened the million-and-a-half abortions that take place in the United States each year to the Holocaust (the murder of millions of Jews and others deemed undesirable and unwanted by Nazi Germany). Some of these activists mean literally that America's "abortuaries" are comparable to the Nazi death camps, a notion that many people—pro-choice, anti-abortion, Jewish, and Christian—find deeply offensive. Other anti-abortion activists use Holocaust imagery to illustrate why we need to value all life, potential as well as actual. A society that casually accepts abortion, they argue, becomes callous toward life and risks "sliding down the slippery slope" toward creating another society like Nazi Germany.

In contrast, most Christians—and even most U.S. Catholics—don't believe abortion should be illegal and do believe abortion is morally justified under some circumstances. Christian positions on abortion are diverse and nuanced, just as Christian denominations in the United States are diverse.

Here's a sampling:

Episcopal Church
We regard all abortion as having a tragic dimension, calling for the concern and compassion of all the Christian community. While we acknowledge that in this country it is the legal right of every woman to have a medically safe abortion, as Christians we believe strongly that

if this right is exercised, it should be used only in extreme situations. We emphatically oppose abortion as a means of birth control, family planning, sex selection or any reason of mere convenience. In those cases where an abortion is being considered, members of this Church are urged to seek the dictates of their conscience in prayer, to seek the advice and counsel of members of the Christian community, and, where appropriate, the sacramental life of this Church.

American Friends Service Committee (Quakers)

For two decades the AFSC has taken a consistent position supporting a woman's right to follow her own conscience concerning childbearing, abortion and sterilization. AFSC is aware that the decision to terminate a pregnancy is seldom easy. That choice must be made free of coercion, including the coercion of poverty, racial discrimination and unavailability of services to those who cannot pay.

Presbyterian Church

The church's position on public policy concerning abortion should reflect respect for other religious traditions and advocacy for full exercise of religious liberty. The Presbyterian Church exists within a very pluralistic environment. Its own members hold a variety of views. It is exactly this pluralism of beliefs which leads us to the conviction that the decision regarding abortion must remain with the individual, to be made on the basis of conscience and personal religious principles, and free from governmental interference.

United Methodist Church
Our belief in the sanctity of human life makes us reluctant to approve abortion. But we are equally bound to respect the sacredness of life and well-being of the mother for whom devastating damage may result from an unacceptable pregnancy. . . . We reject the simplistic answers to the problem of abortion which, on the one hand, regard all abortions as murders, or, on the other hand, regard all abortions as procedures without moral significance. . . . We support the legal right to abortion. . . . We encourage women in counsel with husbands, doctors, and pastors to make their own responsible decisions concerning the personal or moral questions surrounding the issue of abortion.[12]

Religions other than Christianity grapple with the abortion issue, too. Most Muslims today seem to believe that abortion is morally acceptable before "ensoulment" (forty to one hundred twenty days after conception, depending on local or national tradition). Some Muslims, however, believe that all abortion, and even all contraception, is infanticide.[13]

Similarly, some Jews (Orthodox Jews especially) believe that all abortion is sinful and should be prohibited. Most of American Judaism, however, is more flexible on the issue. Two rabbis explain:

The [Jewish] legal codes and rabbinic teachings tend to depict the fetus as simply part of a woman's body. Just as one may not wantonly mutilate one's own body, so, too, a woman is not permitted to obtain an abortion merely for reasons of convenience. But just as she is permitted to sacrifice a portion of her body for her greater good, so, too, may she obtain permission for an abortion in order to assure her overall well-being. The fetus is not a person; it has no rights. Questions of ensoulment, while interesting, are essentially irrelevant. Thus, abortion becomes permissible, according to the vast majority of [Jewish] authorities, under a wide variety of circumstances.

However, it must also be said that Judaism as a religious heritage does not tilt absolutely to one side of any issue. Callousness as to the seriousness and the tragedy of an abortion is unacceptable. Abortion as birth control is unacceptable. Abortion as a means of avoiding the responsibility of bearing children is antithetical to Jewish values.

One final point. Due to the general leniency in matters of abortion, as well as to a long-standing Jewish insistence on the separation of religion and government in American life, all three non-Orthodox Jewish movements—Reform, Reconstructionist and Conservative—are on record opposing any governmental regulation of abortions. Moreover, many Orthodox authorities take the same position. Whatever their opinions on abortion in any given situation, a vast majority of Jewish thinkers agree that decision making with respect to abortion must be left in the hands of the woman involved, her husband, her physician, and her rabbi.[14]

Whatever their official positions on abortion, most religious organizations include individuals who strongly disapprove of abortion as well as those who are convinced that abortion is in many cases a morally correct choice. Furthermore, many who morally disapprove of abortion are convinced that abortion should nonetheless be legal regardless of its morality.

Many religious supporters of legal abortion emphasize that theirs is a compassionate stance. According to one Presbyterian minister:

> Life for a Christian is more than breathing in and out. Until people have a home in which to raise their children, the safety and security of whatever they need to do that well, then abortion needs to be a choice. Clearly, giving a woman the right to abortion is a compassionate stand, and anytime compassion rules over judgment, we see the kingdom of God.
>
> I can't get any of these Bible-thumping, anti-abortion people to show me any place in all Scripture where Jesus ever says, 'You made your bed, now lie in it. Too bad.' . . .
>
> I see Jesus being outrageously gracious, outrageously forgiving. If Jesus were right here today, I think he would say, 'I'm sad that anyone has to have an abortion. I'm sad that has to be a choice. But you've been created as human beings . . . you're going to make mistakes. Yes, I do value life, I do value babies, but I don't use babies for punishment. And you've had a lot of babies born that you haven't taken care of very well. I want you to find homes for these children that have been battered and abused. I want you to get these

people off the streets. I want you to take care of what you've already got.' [15]

One committed Christian who herself has had an abortion describes her experience:

> Having an abortion seemed to be the most thoughtful and loving decision we could make, in fact, it seemed to be the only decision we could make which would still maintain our life goals and plans in helping serve others as we had hoped. I was a Christian then, as I am now, and constant prayer asking for guidance through peace is how I was able to feel that God guided me toward that decision, also. Since the abortion in 1977, I have helped hundreds of emotionally disturbed children, counseled twice as many parents about the loving ways of parenting, become known as the expert in the field of counseling children and families traumatized by sexual abuse, and in 1979 I married a pediatrician who has been a wonderful husband and father. . . . God has given me many blessings and much peace since 1977. [16]

A great many religiously thoughtful people are uncomfortable with both typical pro-choice arguments and anti-abortion positions. Ruth Colker, a feminist theological and legal theorist, explains her disappointment with the way abortion is usually discussed:

> Although I still consider myself to be a pro-choice feminist, I am troubled by three common pro-choice arguments. First, I am disappointed that pro-choice arguments often seem

disrespectful of the seriousness of the pro-life position. Second, I am disappointed that pro-choice arguments tend to focus almost exclusively on the abortion issue while losing sight of the larger context of reproductive health. Third, I am disappointed that the pro-choice position is usually defended on privacy grounds rather than on equality grounds. In my own pro-choice position, I have tried to develop an equality perspective that is respectful of all the lives involved in the abortion decision. . . . I do not try to pretend, however, that the abortion decision is a private decision that only affects the lives of women.

I am also troubled by three common pro-life positions: First, I am disappointed that pro-life advocates are often willing to use the criminal law to regulate abortion. Second, I am disappointed that pro-life advocates also ignore the context of reproductive health; hence, they are often willing to provide virtually no public funding for reproductive health services for poor women even when their health or well-being is substantially threatened by a pregnancy. Third, I am disappointed that pro-life arguments often ignore entirely the lives of the women who bear and raise children, as well as the existing offspring of these women. All of these positions . . . are not tenable to a pro-life perspective that truly respects the lives of women and children.[17]

Related Moral Issues. There are more moral issues concerning abortion than the obvious question of whether an individual should have one. The circumstances in which abortions take place can make resolving these issues more difficult. It may be difficult, for example, to come to terms with the moral implications of having had an abortion if you have to hide what you have done. Broadcast journalist Linda Ellerbee had two abortions—an illegal one, in 1965, when she was young and unmarried and unable to support a child, and another one years later, when she was in her thirties and wanted the child she was carrying but learned that it was badly damaged and likely already dead. "Having the legal abortion was so totally different from having the illegal one. It was inexpensive. It was done in a clinic, a Planned Parenthood clinic, under sterile circumstances, with counseling, and I was not made to feel worse than I already felt. I was helped in grieving my loss, and it was a loss. *Both* times it was a loss."[18]

Pro-choice advocates question whether some of the state-imposed restrictions that the Supreme Court has decreed legally, constitutionally permissible are nonetheless wrong and unethical. Is it ethical, for example, to compel a pregnant, emotionally vulnerable teenager to tell a judge intimate details about her sexual behavior so that she can avoid telling them to a parent she fears? On the other hand, is it ethical to conspire with a teenager to hide her pregnancy from her parents? Do these questions have different answers if the pregnancy is the result of rape or incest? What if the teenager is nearly eighteen years old? What if she's only thirteen?

The issue of public funding for abortions has moral implications as well. The Hyde amendment perpetuates a gap between economic classes that existed long before *Roe:* Wealthier women have always been better able to purchase safer abortions. Abortion, however, is tied up with medical care and not simply a consumer good. Most Americans believe that all Americans should have access to decent medical care whether they can afford

Religious organizations, as well as their individual members, differ in their attitudes about abortion. Many, supporting free will and concerned about the safety of women, support the legality of abortion.

to pay its full cost or not. Is it wrong to refuse to fund medically safe abortions for poor women?

Some of the questions raised by the abortion issue have far-reaching legal and social implications. For example: If a fetus is in some sense a person, what are its rights? If a pregnant woman conducts herself in ways that might damage the fetus, should she be charged with child abuse? In several states, women who abuse drugs have been arrested on just such grounds. On the same grounds, would it be reasonable to prohibit all pregnant women from drinking alcohol? From smoking? Should pregnant women be legally compelled to take vitamins and see a doctor regularly? Prohibited from working at a job where they might be exposed to substances, such as lead, that could harm the fetus? (One Wisconsin factory banned *all* women of childbearing age from jobs that exposed them to lead, to prevent possible birth defects.[19]) What if someone physically harms a pregnant woman, causing her to spontaneously abort? Is that a homicide?

Even U.S. foreign policy must wrestle with moral questions about abortion. U.S. funding for family planning programs abroad, many of which offer abortion services, has long been controversial, and for this reason birth control in foreign countries receives little funding from the U.S. government. Closer to home, the Bush administration in the early 1990s advocated that Chinese citizens fleeing abortions forced upon them by China's strict one-child-per-family policy should be allowed entry into the United States as refugees.

For medical professionals, moral issues connected with abortion persist even after the procedure has been performed. The most obvious such issue is that of using tissue from aborted fetuses for medical research. Fetal tissue, which has unique biological properties, has been useful in the development of vaccines and is in demand for promising research into transplant therapy and treatments for Parkinson's disease, Alzheimer's disease, cancer, AIDS, and other diseases. Federal funding for medical research using fetal tissue from elective abortions has been prohibited since the Reagan administration suspended it in 1988. The ban was lifted early in the Clinton administration, but the issue has remained controversial. (Anti-abortion advocates have urged using fetal tissue from miscarriages and ectopic pregnancies as an alternative to tissue from elective abortions. Researchers reported in January 1995, however, that such tissue is typically diseased or genetically abnormal, and so is only rarely suitable for transplant therapy.[20])

The moral complexity of abortion has made it a hotly debated issue in the United States, and diverse groups of activists seek to influence individual decision making as well as public policy on abortion.

6

The Activists

Dozens of organizations concerned about abortion are active in the United States. They differ not only in their attitudes toward abortion, but also in their tactics and approaches to the issue. These are some of the better-known groups of pro-choice and anti-abortion activists. Each group, through its own literature, speaks for itself.

National Abortion Federation. The National Abortion Federation (NAF) is first and foremost a trade association: "a nonprofit, professional association of abortion providers—representing physicians, nurses, administrators, counselors, and other medical staff at over 300 abortion facilities in the United States and Canada." NAF provides training and continuing medical education, sets professional standards for abortion care, and offers "everything from liability insurance to legal assistance, from a computerized reference library to Congressional representation, from discounts on supplies to data on new medical products."

NAF also operates a national toll-free hotline for women seeking abortion services. Women who call this

800-number receive information about abortion and are referred to an abortion provider near them.

As "the voice of abortion providers and a source of accurate and unbiased information for legislators and policymakers, medical groups, the media, and the public," NAF publishes various educational materials and lobbies to keep abortion legal and accessible and to keep clinics safe from anti-abortion violence.[1]

National Abortion and Reproductive Rights Action League. Founded in 1969, when abortion was by and large illegal in the United States, NARAL first lobbied, organized, and advocated for making abortion legal and has since worked to ensure that abortion remains a safe and legal option for women. NARAL, a national organization with more than half a million members, lobbies Congress and state legislatures, presents legal briefs in abortion-related court cases, and advocates for abortion rights in the press. In recent years, according to its literature, it has focused on "combating violence and the anti-choice, radical right movement." And it has begun to broaden its focus beyond abortion to "reproductive choices" more generally, seeking "to promote policies that will make abortion less necessary. We must ensure," says NARAL, "that state and national policies enable women and men to make responsible, deliberate decisions about sexuality, contraception, pregnancy, childbirth and abortion."[2]

National Conference of Catholic Bishops' Secretariat for Pro-Life Activities. This is the official voice of the U.S. Catholic Church on the abortion issue. According to a resolution adopted by the bishops in 1989: "As leaders of the Catholic community in the United States, we acknowledge our right and responsibility to help establish laws and social policies protecting the right to life of unborn children." According to its literature, the bishops' public policy goals include:

- constitutional protection for the right to life of unborn children to the maximum degree possible;
- federal and state laws and administrative policies that restrict support for and the practice of abortion;
- continual refinement and ultimate reversal of Supreme Court and other court decisions that deny the inalienable right to life;
- supportive legislation to provide morally acceptable alternatives to abortion, and social policy initiatives which provide support to pregnant women for prenatal care and extended support for low-income women and their children.

In addition to broadcasting the Catholic Church's views on abortion through the American press, the Bishops' Secretariat for Pro-Life Activities publishes its own educational materials concerning abortion.[3]

National Right to Life (including National Teens for Life). According to its literature:
National Right to Life, the nation's largest pro-life group, works to protect innocent human lives threatened by abortion, infanticide and euthanasia. National Right to Life works to restore protection for human life through the work of:

- the National Right to Life Committee (NRLC), which provides leadership, communications, organizational, lobbying and legislative work on both the federal and state level;
- the National Right to Life Political Action Committee (NRL-PAC), a nonpartisan political action committee, which works to elect, on the state and federal level, officials who respect democracy's most precious right: the right to life;
- various outreach efforts to groups affected by society's lack of respect for human life: the disability rights community, the post-abortion community, the Hispanic and African-American communities and the community of faith;
- *NRL News,* NRLC's biweekly newspaper, which prints a variety of news and commentary of interest to the pro-life community.

One of National Right to Life's "outreach efforts" is National Teens for Life, which describes itself as "our generation's response to the abortion holocaust." Since 1985, local Teens for Life groups have been founded across the United States. According to its national office, their activities include "speaking in schools and to youth groups, volunteering in crisis pregnancy centers, peer counseling, debating, and helping adult right-to-life groups pass pro-life legislation."[4]

Operation Rescue. Founded by Randall Terry, a young man who became a "born again" Christian in the late 1970s and who saw "saving babies from the death chamber" as his mission, Operation Rescue by 1988 had recruited nearly 100,000 activists.[5] By then, Operation

Rescue was frequently in the news as it targeted abortion clinics in particular cities for blockade actions: Activists gathered at a targeted clinic in sufficient numbers to prevent anyone from entering the building, refused to move, and were carried off by the police one by one—a time-consuming and expensive operation. The group called these actions "rescues." According to Operation Rescue's literature:

> A rescue is a group of God-fearing people peacefully putting themselves between the killer (abortionist) and his intended victims (the baby and the mother). To rescue someone is to physically intervene on their behalf when they are in danger. We have an obligation before God to try to rescue these children and these women. We do this in a spirit of repentance for our many years of apathy and lack of action. Christians who do rescue missions are simply obeying God's command to rescue the innocent who are scheduled to die that day, regardless of man's ungodly law that permits and protects murder.[6]

Operation Rescue preaches nonviolence. Nonetheless, many pro-choice activists believe that its provocative language has been taken as encouragement by anti-abortion terrorists.

Operation Rescue's acts of civil disobedience have landed many of its members in court, where expensive judgments often have been handed down against them. The group has moved its headquarters and changed its leadership several times in recent years. Randall Terry has remained an active advisor to the organization, featuring prominently in its literature.

In August 1995, in a swimming pool in Dallas, Texas, Flip Benham, national director of Operation Rescue, baptized Norma McCorvey, known as Jane Roe, as a "born again" Christian.

In early 1995, Operation Rescue moved its national headquarters right next door to a Dallas abortion clinic that employed Norma McCorvey, a.k.a. "Jane Roe." ("At the killing center, at the gates of hell, is where the church of Jesus Christ needs to be," said Flip Benham, Operation Rescue's director.[7]) In August 1995, Benham baptized McCorvey as a "born again" Christian. McCorvey announced she had come to believe that abortion was morally wrong, although she still felt it should be legally available in the first trimester.

Planned Parenthood volunteer Lisa Maas cheers over the news that the clinic remained open throughout the day of Pope John Paul II's 1993 visit to Denver, despite the picketing of anti-abortion protesters.

Planned Parenthood. Planned Parenthood is best known for its network of hundreds of clinics that provide birth control, abortion services, and other reproductive health care. According to its mission statement:

> Planned Parenthood believes in the fundamental right of each individual, throughout the world, to manage his or her fertility, regardless of the individual's income, marital status, age, national origin, or residence. We believe that reproductive self-determination must be voluntary and preserve the individual's right to privacy. We further believe that such self-determination will contribute to an enhancement of the quality of life, strong family relationships, and population stability.

> Based on these beliefs, the mission of Planned Parenthood is:

> - to provide comprehensive reproductive and complementary health care services in settings which preserve and protect the essential privacy and rights of each individual;
> - to advocate public policies which guarantee these rights and ensure access to such services;
> - to provide educational programs which enhance understanding of individual and societal implications of human sexuality;
> - to promote research and advancement of technology in reproductive health care and encourage understanding of their inherent bioethical, behavioral, and social implications.

In 1993, Planned Parenthood centers "provided medical services to nearly 2.4 million clients," including more than 134,000 women who sought and received abortion services.

Planned Parenthood also establishes medical guidelines for its clinics, promotes research into improved methods of contraception, seeks to educate the public about sexuality and reproduction issues, and advocates government policies favoring family planning in both the United States and abroad.[8]

Pro-Life Action League. Founded in 1980 by longtime anti-abortion activist Joe Scheidler, the Pro-Life Action League describes its goal as "saving babies' lives through non-violent direct action." Best known for organizing and inspiring pickets and acts of civil disobedience such as sit-ins designed to shut down abortion clinics, the Pro-Life Action League also facilitates and encourages other forms of anti-abortion activism. According to its literature:

> Activism takes many forms, from sidewalk counseling to picketing to rescue missions at abortion clinics. . . . We recruit activist leaders in every city to carry out the effective program we are using. . . .
>
> We conduct seminars and conferences, lecture before student groups, speak at pro-life rallies, and debate at leading universities. The League helps pro-life activists organize effective programs, trains them to become successful pro-life leaders in their communities and save lives through direct action. . . .
>
> We try to make it difficult for those who profit from abortion to exercise their lethal trade.

A member of the Pro-Life Action Ministries, an anti-choice organization in Minnesota, protests the installation of an eight-foot-high fence around the only Planned Parenthood clinic in the state that provides abortions.

The Pro-Life Action League is a relatively small organization, but it is influential among anti-abortion activists and gets a lot of press coverage for its confrontational, megaphone-at-the-clinic-door tactics. In early 1995, its active donor list numbered about 8,000, and its annual operating budget was about $400,000.

Although the organization's literature preaches nonviolence, many pro-choice activists believe that its networking among radical anti-abortion groups has encouraged if not actually aided the perpetrators of anti-abortion violence. Certainly Joe Scheidler's book, *CLOSED: 99 Ways to Stop Abortion,* has encouraged many activists to take a more confrontational approach to abortion.[9]

Religious Coalition for Reproductive Choice. The Religious Coalition for Reproductive Choice (RCRC), formerly the Religious Coalition for Abortion Rights, is made up of more than three dozen Christian, Jewish, and other religious organizations (from mainstream denominations such as the Presbyterian Church to groups that speak for themselves but not their churches, such as Catholics for a Free Choice). It has more than fifty organizing chapters throughout the United States. RCRC's purpose, according to its mission statement, "is to ensure that every woman is free to make decisions about when to have children according to her own conscience and religious beliefs, without government interference. The Coalition's primary role is to make clear that abortion can be a moral, ethical, and religiously responsible decision."

Founded in 1973 in response to religiously based efforts to overturn *Roe* v. *Wade* and to make abortion illegal once again, the coalition's constituent groups together represent millions of individuals with diverse religious perspectives and diverse views on the morality of abortion. What unifies them is a strong and clear belief that laws prohibiting abortion seriously violate religious liberty. According to its literature:

> Because each denomination and faith group represented among us approaches the issue of abortion from the unique perspective of its own theology, members hold widely varying viewpoints as to when abortion is morally justified. This plurality of beliefs leads us to the

conviction that the abortion decision must remain with the individual, to be made on the basis of conscience and personal religious principles, and free from government interference.

[RCRC] opposes any attempts to enact into secular law restrictions on abortion rights based on one theological definition of when a fetus becomes a human being.

We hold in high respect the value of potential human life and do not take the question of abortion lightly. [RCRC] members believe it is important for the religious community to provide leadership and guidance on the moral and ethical aspects of this sensitive issue.

RCRC works primarily through public education, teaching about religious rationales for pro-choice positions through the press and through its own educational publications.[10]

Voters for Choice. A political action committee, Voters for Choice collects money from pro-choice donors and contributes to the political campaigns of candidates who support abortion rights. According to the organization:

Voters for Choice contributes to pro-choice candidates running for the U.S. Senate, House of Representatives, governor, and for state legislatures.

Voters for Choice is bipartisan and independent. We assist Democrats and Republicans, incumbents and challengers. We help candidates in primary and general elections.

Contributors to Voters for Choice know that their funds are strategically directed to the most important, most pivotal electoral campaigns in the country—the campaigns that will assure that abortion is maintained as a safe, legal, and accessible choice for the women of America.

Voters for Choice takes credit for having "helped elect and reelect more than 175 Members of Congress" in the 1980s and early 1990s. In addition to funneling contributions of money to pro-choice candidates, Voters for Choice offers candidates technical assistance with fundraising, polling, and media relations; advises candidates on campaign strategy; alerts potential donors about key electoral races; and advises voters about candidates' positions on abortion.[11]

7

Outside the Courts Since Roe *v.* Wade

For those who say I can't impose my morality on others, I say just watch me.

Joe Scheidler[1]

In the mid-1970s, just as anti-abortion activism in response to *Roe* v. *Wade* was taking off, right-wing Republican party activists stepped up efforts to reach out to socially conservative voters concerned about what they perceived as a decline in American family life and morality. As these right-wing activists nudged aside the more moderate Republicans who had long dominated the party's leadership, the social, "pro-family" issues that concerned these conservative voters (such as prayer in schools and opposition to recognizing the rights of women and homosexuals) became key elements of the party's appeal. Opposition to abortion was one such element, and it helped draw many of the growing numbers of "born again" conservative evangelical Christians as well as Catholic right-to-lifers into politics, and into an alliance with the Republican "new right."

In 1980, socially conservative activists helped sweep a wave of anti-abortion Republican candidates into office, including their preferred candidate for the presidency, Ronald Reagan. Although the new, more conservative Congress failed to enact a proposed amendment to the U.S. Constitution that would have banned abortion by asserting that human life begins at conception, the anti-abortion agenda was pressed ahead during the Reagan and Bush presidencies by the White House and by state and local governments across the nation.

Behind the scenes, Reagan appointees made federal agencies as diverse as the Office of Personnel Management and the Centers for Disease Control hostile to any dissent from a strict anti-abortion position. More publicly, Reagan's surgeon general C. Everett Koop became a familiar anti-abortion spokesman. Koop explicitly linked abortion in any form to such morally indefensible activities as the eugenics policies—from forced sterilization to concentration camps—practiced by Nazi Germany.[2]

Other anti-abortion activists, within and outside the government, insisted that abortion on demand was not far removed from abortion on *command*—compulsory abortion at the command of the state, as practiced for example by China in pursuit of its one-child-per-family population-control policy. Pro-choice activists bristled at this analogy, countering that in both cases the issue was *choice*—that individual women everywhere should be free to choose when and whether to bear children.

Although clearly unfriendly to legalized abortion, the Reagan administration presided over few lasting changes in federal law on the issue. One contentious change was the "gag rule" forbidding doctors and counselors working at family-planning facilities receiving federal funding from providing information about abortion or referring patients to abortion providers. But pro-choice activists and many medical professionals denounced the rule as bad medicine and an improper intrusion into the relationship between doctors and patients. Enacted in 1987, the gag rule was promptly challenged in federal court, then upheld by the Supreme Court in 1991.

By then Reagan was no longer president, but the anti-abortion policies favored during his administration continued to be pursued by his successor. George Bush, vice president during the Reagan years, had in the past supported family-planning programs generally and the *Roe* decision in particular. By the time of his successful 1988 presidential campaign, however, his position had become unambiguously anti-abortion:

> I believe that abortion is wrong. I believe that we should work to change *Roe* v. *Wade,* and I pledge to join you in that struggle. Abortion on demand should not be legal. And it won't be—but only if we persevere. . . . This fall [in the presidential election], you've got a very clear choice. Together, we can continue the struggle to protect human life. Or we can turn the Executive Branch over to those for whom this is not a priority.
>
> I intend to persevere. I ask you to join me. And I look forward to joining you as a pro-life president at this time next year.[3]

In January 1989, just days after his inauguration, President Bush addressed by telephone some 65,000 anti-abortion demonstrators in Washington, describing abortion as "an American tragedy."[4] He clearly supported a step taken by the Justice Department shortly before he took office, just two days after he had won the 1988 presidential election. The department had filed a friend-of-the-court brief in an abortion case that the Supreme Court had recently agreed to review, suggesting that "if the Supreme Court is prepared to reconsider *Roe* v. *Wade,* this case presents an appropriate opportunity for doing so."[5] The case in question was *Webster* v. *Reproductive Health Services.*

Pro-choice activists mobilized in opposition to the threat posed by the case. Several months later, on April 9, 1989, while the Court was still considering *Webster,* hundreds of thousands of demonstrators marched from the Washington Monument past the Supreme Court building to the U.S. Capitol, demanding that the legal right to choose abortion be kept and defended.

The *Webster* decision, handed down by the Supreme Court in July, pleased neither pro-choice nor anti-abortion activists. Anti-abortion advocates were disappointed that the Supreme Court had not, as they had hoped, taken the opportunity to strike down *Roe* once and for all. They were encouraged, however, that the Missouri law restricting abortions had been approved. Activists resolved to press forward with introducing and lobbying for anti-abortion laws in state legislatures across the country—laws designed, as one Pennsylvania legislator phrased it, to permit the Supreme Court "to either overturn *Roe* v. *Wade* in its entirety or to continue the erosion process begun under *Webster.*"[6] Literally hundreds of anti-abortion laws have been introduced in state legislatures across the country since *Webster;* most have not been passed.

Pro-choicers, too, were nudged into action by *Webster.* Since *Roe,* the law of the land had been on their side. The *Webster* decision indicated that *Roe* couldn't

The March for Life culminates in an anti-abortion demonstration at the Supreme Court. The march takes place each year on the anniversary of Roe v. Wade.

be taken for granted. Prodded by pro-choice activists, a few state legislatures since *Webster* have passed laws protecting legal access to abortion. Pro-choicers after *Webster* also became more active than they had been in previous years in supporting pro-choice political candidates, who gained ground in the 1990 elections.[7]

During the Reagan and Bush administrations, abortion became an entrenched political issue in the United States. With both anti-abortion and pro-choice activists mobilized and politically active, abortion became a "litmus test" by which every judicial or political appointee—and every elected politician—would be judged. Nominees for the Supreme Court have been scrutinized especially closely for indications of how they might approach abortion cases.

Judicial appointments generally may well be the strongest and most lasting anti-abortion legacy of the Reagan and Bush presidencies. During their twelve years in office, these two presidents filled five of the nine seats on the Supreme Court (Justices Sandra Day O'Connor, Antonin Scalia, Anthony Kennedy, David Souter, and Clarence Thomas). Presidents Reagan and Bush also appointed their choices to a majority of all federal and district court judgeships. Most of these were conservative jurists who were expected to oppose abortion, and many were young men who would serve in these life appointments for many years to come.

In 1992, U.S. voters elected a pro-choice president, Bill Clinton, who campaigned on the position that abortion should be "safe, legal, and rare." Well before Clinton was elected, anti-abortion violence—arson, vandalism, assault, and even murder—had begun to escalate, and the new administration vowed to respond aggressively to the violence.

In 1993, the U.S. Justice Department created a Task Force on Violence Against Abortion Providers to look for links among incidents of anti-abortion violence, which have been scattered around the country, and to determine whether or not they are part of a hidden illegal conspiracy to put abortion providers out of business. The task force was strengthened and its work intensified after Paul Hill's shootings in Pensacola.

In May 1994, President Clinton signed into law the Freedom of Access to Clinic Entrances Act, which made it a federal offense to block access or damage property at clinics, or to injure or threaten or interfere with clinic staff or patients. By January 1995, the Justice Department had filed four civil actions against anti-abortion activists under the act. The lawsuits sought to impose fines and restraining orders against activists ac-

Pro-choice demonstrators during a rally of the National Organization for Women outside the Houston Astrodome on August 15, 1992, as Republicans prepare for their national convention.

cused of blocking entrances to abortion clinics and harassing clinic employees.[8]

Anti-abortion activists have complained that enforcement of the Freedom of Access to Clinic Entrances Act could infringe their First Amendment right to freedom of speech. (The Supreme Court rejected this argument, in *Woodall* v. *Reno,* in June 1995.) Pro-choice advocates say that the act won't be enough to stop the violence; in fact, violence at clinics has continued.

Anti-abortion groups have routinely condemned anti-abortion violence, but many pro-choice activists have felt that the condemnations of some of the more radical groups have been far from convincing. Operation Rescue, especially, has been widely criticized for using incendiary rhetoric that nominally condemns violence while seeming to tacitly accept it. For example, Operation Rescue's director wrote in a letter to the group's supporters at the end of 1994:

> The abortion industry is crumbling under the weight of its own sin. . . . God Himself is raining the consequences of child killing upon the heads of those who do such things to His precious image bearers. His consequences are also falling upon a nation that approves of such barbarism. Whether or not the pro-life movement existed at all, the child killing industry would still be running into the face of Almighty God. Killing children is a losing proposition no matter how you look at it. The entire abortion industry is teetering on the brink of collapse. It is reaping the horrible consequences of what it has sown. . . .
>
> Now is the time to press on toward the goal set before us. We are not concerned that child killing becomes illegal, though we believe that will be a by product of our faithfulness. We do not see the victory in the murder of child killers, though we understand, but do not tolerate, the frustration that drives some to take matters into their own hands. We believe, we know, we abide in the fact that Truth will overcome the lie; that Light will cast out darkness; that victory is our Lord's.[9]

Four days after this letter was dated, on December 30, 1994, John C. Salvi III opened fire and killed two employees at two abortion clinics in Massachusetts.

Aside from the Freedom of Access act, abortion was mostly a back-burner issue during the early years of the Clinton administration. The issue of insurance coverage for abortion arose but was not resolved during the 1993–1994 discussions of legislation for national health-care reform. The administration's most prolonged, high-profile wrangle with the abortion issue came, surprisingly, with the nomination of Henry Foster to be U.S. surgeon general. Foster, an obstetrician-gynecologist who had occasionally performed abortions as a relatively small part of his private medical practice, became a lightning rod for anti-abortion rhetoric. His nomination died in the Senate in June 1995.

By then, the 1994 congressional elections had brought not only Republican majorities to both houses of Congress, but also a majority or near-majority of members expected to vote in favor of various anti-abortion measures—should they come to a vote. Republican leaders, however, had sought to avoid raising the abortion issue (as well as other divisive social issues) during the new Congress's first 100 days, so that they could concentrate on legislation related to the "Contract with America" they had promoted during the fall 1994 electoral campaign. When the abortion issue *did* arise, positions on it didn't simply follow party lines. In early 1995, for example, many anti-abortion conservatives in and out of the U.S. Congress allied with liberal Democrats in opposing Republican-backed efforts to deny welfare benefits to many pregnant women. These welfare-reform restrictions, they argued, could encourage women to have abortions instead of carrying their pregnancies to term.

While Republicans in Congress concentrated on the "Contract," the politically active religious right, which claimed credit for electing many of the new Republican congressmen, waited with growing impatience and concern for "their" Congress to aggressively pursue a conservative social agenda including opposition to abortion rights. They had reason to be concerned. With an eye to appealing to a broader range of voters in the 1996 presidential election, Republican party leadership by early 1995 was considering "balancing" its ticket with a moderately pro-choice vice-presidential candidate as well as deleting or moderating the tough anti-abortion plank in the party's platform, both as part of a general move toward a more moderate stance on social issues. In February 1995, Ralph Reed, executive director of the Christian Coalition (a powerful lobbying and get-out-the-vote organization that pursues a conservative public policy agenda), pointedly warned that anti-abortion voters would desert the Republican party if its nominee for either president or vice president in 1996 was pro-choice on abortion.[10]

The Republican party clearly didn't want to lose the votes of the religious right. On the other hand, one early Republican presidential candidate, Senator Arlen Specter of Pennsylvania, echoed the views of many moderate voters when he laid out a clear Republican rationale for his pro-choice position:

> I want to take abortion out of politics. I want to keep the Republican party focused on the critical social, economic, military, foreign policy, and crime control issues and leave moral issues such as abortion to the conscience of the individual. That is a matter to be decided by women, not by big government. Neither this

The moral, legal, and ethical issues of abortion continue to divide the country, in heated and sometimes violent debates, privately and publicly.

nation nor this party can afford a Republican candidate so captive to the demands of the intolerant right that we end up by re-electing a president of the incompetent left.[11]

It appeared inevitable that—whether party leadership wanted it or not—the abortion issue would continue to influence U.S. politics strongly in 1996 and beyond.

For decades, public-opinion polls have consistently shown that most Americans believe that abortion should be legally available. At the same time, most Americans believe that abortion is in many circumstances morally wrong. This widespread ambivalence about abortion has spilled over into a great many areas of public debate: national politics, constitutional law, health-care provision, church and state. Meanwhile, as the public debate has grown louder and more heated and even violent, abortion has also quietly and directly touched the private lives of millions of American women and men. Controversy about public policy—and private choices—on abortion is far from resolution and will likely persist for many years to come.

Notes

Chapter One
Violence and Controversy

1. *Washington Post,* December 31, 1994.
2. Judy Widdicombe, excerpted from Anna Bonavoglia's *The Choices We Made: Twenty-five Women and Men Speak Out About Abortion* (New York: Random House, 1991), pp. 132–133.

Chapter Two
Before **Roe** *v.* **Wade**

1. Roger Rosenblatt, *Life Itself: Abortion in the American Mind* (New York: Random House, 1992), pp. 84–85.
2. Margaret Sanger, *My Fight for Birth Control* (New York: Farrar-Rinehart, 1931), excerpted from Alice S. Rossi, ed., *The Feminist Papers: From Adams to de Beauvoir* (New York: Bantam, 1974), p. 523.
3. May 1989 interview with unnamed woman, quoted in Catherine Whitney, *Whose Life? A Balanced, Comprehensive View of Abortion from Its Historical Context to the Current Debate* (New York: Morrow, 1991), p. 49.
4. Judy Widdicombe, excerpted from *The Choices We Made,* p. 124.
5. Grace Paley, excerpted from *The Choices We Made,* p. 6.
6. Barbara Corday, excerpted from *The Choices We Made,* pp. 74, 76.
7. Grace Paley, excerpted from *The Choices We Made,* p. 8.
8. Boston Women's Health Book Collective, *The New Our Bodies,*

Ourselves: A Book by and for Women (New York: Simon and Schuster, 1992), p. 373.

9. *Life Itself*, pp. 92–93.
10. *Griswold* v. *Connecticut* (1965).
11. *Eisenstadt* v. *Baird* (1972).

Chapter Three
The Law Since Roe v. Wade

1. *Roe* v. *Wade* (1973).
2. *Danforth* v. *Planned Parenthood of Missouri* (1976).
3. Ruth Colker, *Abortion and Dialogue: Pro-Choice, Pro-Life, and American Law* (Bloomington: Indiana University Press, 1992), p. 85.
4. *Danforth* v. *Planned Parenthood of Missouri* (1976).
5. *Danforth* v. *Planned Parenthood of Missouri* (1976).
6. *Bellotti* v. *Baird* (1979).
7. Quoted in *The New Our Bodies, Ourselves*, p. 354.
8. *Beal* v. *Doe* (1977); *Maher* v. *Roe* (1977).
9. *Poelker* v. *Doe* (1977).
10. Justice Brennan's dissent in *Maher* v. *Roe*, quoted in George J. Annas, *Judging Medicine* (Clifton, NJ: Humana Press, 1988), p. 153.
11. *The New Our Bodies, Ourselves*, p. 377.
12. Quoted in Catherine Whitney, *Whose Life? A Balanced, Comprehensive View of Abortion from Its Historical Context to the Current Debate* (New York: William Morrow, 1991), p. 79.
13. Quoted in *Judging Medicine*, p. 165.
14. *Patricia R. Harris, Secretary of Health and Human Services* v. *Cora McCrae* (1980).
15. Alan Guttmacher Institute, "Facts in Brief: Abortion in the United States," a fact sheet dated August 31, 1994.
16. S. K. Henshaw and L. S. Wallisch, "The Medicaid Cutoff and Abortion Services for the Poor," *Family Planning Perspectives* vol. 16: pp. 170–180 (1984), cited in *Judging Medicine*, p. 157.
17. *Danforth* v. *Planned Parenthood of Missouri* (1976).
18. *Doe* v. *Bolton* (1973).
19. *Danforth* v. *Planned Parenthood of Missouri* (1976).
20. *Akron* v. *Akron Center for Reproductive Health* (1983).
21. *Thornburgh* v. *ACOG* (1986).
22. Justice Blackmun's dissent in the *Webster* case, quoted in *Whose Life?*, p. 124.

Chapter Four
The Medical Picture

1. Guttmacher Institute fact sheet.
2. Quoted in *Whose Life?*, p. 81.
3. *Washington Post*, January 22, 1995.
4. Guttmacher Institute fact sheet.
5. *Washington Post*, January 22, 1995.
6. Guttmacher Institute fact sheet.
7. The information in this section is mostly distilled from various studies cited in *Abortion and Dialogue* and from literature supplied by the Alan Guttmacher Institute.
8. Excerpts from Guttmacher Institute fact sheet, order rearranged.
9. Centers for Disease Control report cited in *Washington Post*, December 24, 1994.
10. *New York Times*, August 31, 1995.
11. Guttmacher Institute fact sheet.
12. Guttmacher Institute fact sheet.
13. Rayna Rapp, excerpted from *The Choices We Made*, p. 160.
14. *The New Our Bodies, Ourselves*, p. 366.
15. Nora Sayre, excerpted from *The Choices We Made*, p. 62.
16. Byllye Avery, excerpted from *The Choices We Made*, pp. 151–152.
17. Quoted in *Abortion and Dialogue*, p. 51.

Chapter Five
Moral Perspectives

1. Quoted in *Whose Life?*, p. 120.
2. Open letter to Bishop B. Austin Vaughan, 1989 or 1990, quoted in *Whose Life?*, p. 161.
3. Interview published in the weekly newspaper *Catholic New York*, quoted in *Whose Life?*, p. 162.
4. Quoted in *Whose Life?*, p. 166.
5. *Life Itself*, pp. 64–67.
6. *Evangelium Vitae*, published on March 30, 1995.
7. Quoted in *Whose Life?*, pp. 170–171.
8. Petition written by Sister Margaret Ellen Traxler and signed by 24 other nuns in 1984, quoted in *The Choices We Made*, p. 192.
9. *Whose Life?*, p. 66.
10. The Reverend Howard Moody, excerpted from *The Choices We Made*, p. 192.

11. National Conference of Catholic Bishops' Committee for Pro-Life Activities, "Abortion: Questions and Answers," an undated pamphlet.

12. All four church statements are excerpted from "We Affirm: National Religious Organizations' Statements on Abortion Rights," an undated pamphlet published by the Religious Coalition for Abortion Rights (now called Religious Coalition for Reproductive Choice).

13. *Life Itself*, p. 79.

14. Rabbi Raymond A. Zwerin and Rabbi Richard J. Shapiro, "Judaism and Abortion," an undated pamphlet published by Religious Coalition for Abortion Rights (now known as Religious Coalition for Reproductive Choice), p. 7.

15. The Reverend Christine Gimbol, excerpted from *The Choices We Made*, pp. 200–201.

16. Quoted in *Abortion and Dialogue*, p. 53.

17. *Abortion and Dialogue*, p. xiv.

18. Linda Ellerbee, excerpted from *The Choices We Made*, p. 87.

19. *Whose Life?*, p. 209.

20. *Washington Post*, January 4, 1995.

Chapter Six
The Activists

1. All information about National Abortion Federation is from a packet of information sent to the author by the organization in February 1995.

2. All information about NARAL is from a packet of information sent to the author by the organization in April 1995.

3. All information about the Secretariat for Pro-Life Activities is from a packet of information sent to the author by the organization in December 1994.

4. All information about National Right to Life and about Teens for Life is from packets of information sent to the author by the organizations in March 1995 and December 1994, respectively.

5. *Whose Life?*, p. 98.

6. "Common Questions About Operation Rescue," an undated pamphlet published by Operation Rescue Dallas/Fort Worth, PO Box 740063, Dallas, TX 75374.

7. *Washington Post*, April 1, 1995.

8. All information about Planned Parenthood is from a packet of information sent to the author by the organization in March 1995.

9. All information about Pro-Life Action League is from two packets of information sent to the author by the organization in December 1994 and March 1995.
10. All information about Religious Coalition for Reproductive Choice is from a packet of information sent to the author by the organization in December 1994.
11. All information about Voters for Choice is from a packet of information sent to the author by the organization in January 1995.

Chapter Seven
Outside the Courts Since Roe *v.* Wade

1. *Pro-Life Action News,* August 8, 1989, quoted in Michele McKeegan, *Abortion Politics: Mutiny in the Ranks of the Right* (New York: Free Press, 1992), p. 111.
2. *Whose Life?,* p. 85, cites an article by Koop on this subject entitled "The Slide to Auschwitz."
3. Written statement from George Bush, 1988, intended for distribution to religious organizations, quoted in *Whose Life?,* p. 33.
4. *Whose Life?,* p. 91.
5. Quoted from *Whose Life?,* pp. 116–117.
6. Stephen Freind, quoted in *Abortion Politics,* p. 144.
7. *Abortion Politics,* p. 153.
8. *Washington Post,* January 19, 1995.
9. Letter from Operation Rescue, December, 1994.
10. *Washington Post,* February 11, 1995.
11. Arlen Specter's March 30, 1995, speech in Washington, DC, announcing his candidacy for the Republican 1996 presidential nomination.

Further
Information

Recommended Reading

Bonavoglia, Anna. *The Choices We Made: Twenty-Five Women and Men Speak Out About Abortion.* New York: Random House, 1991.

Boston Women's Health Book Collective. *The New Our Bodies, Ourselves: A Book by and for Women.* New York: Simon and Schuster, 1992.

Blanchard, Dallas A., and Terry J. Prewitt. *Religious Violence and Abortion: The Gideon Project.* Gainesville: University of Florida Press, 1993.

Colker, Ruth. *Abortion and Dialogue: Pro-Choice, Pro-Life, and American Law.* Bloomington: Indiana University Press, 1992.

Craig, Barbara Hinkson, and David M. O'Brien. *Abortion and American Politics.* Chatham, NJ: Chatham House Publishers, 1993.

McKeegan, Michele. *Abortion Politics: Mutiny in the Ranks of the Right.* New York: Free Press, 1992.

Rosenblatt, Roger. *Life Itself: Abortion in the American Mind.* New York: Random House, 1992.

Organizations to Contact

Alan Guttmacher Institute
120 Wall Street
New York, NY 10005

Catholics for a Free Choice
1436 U Street, NW, Suite 301
Washington, DC 20009

Common Ground Network for Life and Choice
1601 Connecticut Avenue, NW, Suite 200
Washington, DC 20009

National Abortion Federation
1436 U Street, NW, Suite 103
Washington, DC 20009

National Abortion and Reproductive Rights Action League
1156 15th Street, NW, Suite 700
Washington, DC 20005

National Conference of Catholic Bishops'
Secretariat for Pro-Life Activities
3211 4th Street, NE
Washington, DC 20017

National Right to Life and National Teens for Life
419 7th Street, NW, Suite 500
Washington, DC 20004

Operation Rescue National
PO Box 740066
Dallas, TX 75374

Planned Parenthood
810 Seventh Avenue
New York, NY 10019

Pro-Life Action League
6160 N. Cicero Avenue, Suite 600
Chicago, IL 60646

Religious Coalition for Reproductive Choice
1025 Vermont Avenue, NW, Suite 1130
Washington, DC 20005

Voters for Choice
2604 Connecticut Avenue, NW, #200
Washington, DC 20008

Index

14th Amendment to the Constitution, 30
Freedom of Access to Clinic Entrances Act of 1994, 96, 97, 99

Gag rule, 41, 92-93
Griffin, Michael F., 14
Griswold v. *Connecticut* (1965), 27
Gunn, David, 14
Guttmacher Institute, 45, 48, 53

Harris v. *McCrae* (1980), 36-37
Health insurance, 43, 47, 99
Hill, Paul, 14, 96
Hodgson v. *Minnesota* (1990), 41
Holocaust imagery, 67
Husband's consent, 32-33
Hyde, Henry, 36
Hyde amendment, 36-37, 43, 74

Illegal abortions, 11, 18-26, 65
Incest, 26, 37, 48, 74
Induction (instillation) abortion, 54-55
Informed consent, 50
Intrauterine device (IUD), 50, 52

Jane Collective, 26
John Paul II, Pope, 63
Judaism, 62, 69-70
Judicial appointments, 41, 95-96

Kennedy, Anthony, 96
Koop, C. Everett, 92

Lowney, Shannon Elizabeth, 9
Lutherans, 65

Maas, Lisa, *84*
Maguire, David, 63-64
March for Life, *95*
McCorvey, Norma, 28, *29, 40,* 83
Medicaid, 36, 37, 47
Methotrexate, 51

Misprostol, 51
Mormons, 65
Morning-after pill, 50
Muslims, 69

Nathanson, Bernard, 44-45
National Abortion and Reproductive Rights Action League (NARAL), 44, 79
National Abortion Federation (NAF), 78-79
National Conference of Catholic Bishops, 65, 67
Secretariat for Pro-Life Activities, 79-80
National Organization for Women, 97
National Right to Life, 80-83
National Teens for Life, 80, 81
Nichols, Leanne, 9

O'Connor, John J., 62
O'Connor, Sandra Day, 96
Ohio v. *Akron Center for Reproductive Health* (1990), 41
Operation Rescue, 65, *66,* 81-83, 98

Paley, Grace, 23, 25
Parental notification, 34-35, 41, 42, 49, 74
Pius IX, Pope, 63
Planned Parenthood clinics, 9, *58, 84,* 85-86, *87*
Planned Parenthood v. *Casey* (1992), 42
Pregnancy tests, 49
Presbyterian Church, 68-69, 71, 88
Preterm Health Services Clinic, Massachusetts, 9
Privacy, right of, 11, 27, 30-32, 35, 73
Pro-Life Action League, 12, 86-87
Psychological effects of abortion, 55-57, 59